Praise for *Stock Footage Millionaire*

"*Stock Footage Millionaire* is, by far, the most complete guide to producing stock footage published to date. If you are a stock footage producer, pay attention to this. Robb has written a detailed recipe for success that I know works well."

—Jim Goertz (aka VCR), Director, Video Content Development, iStockphoto

"Anyone who calls themselves a videographer or cinematographer should read this book. As someone who works with thousands of stock footage contributors, this book is a comprehensive layout of what one must learn and do to become a top stock footage earner. From purchasing equipment, to preproduction, field production and postproduction, *Stock Footage Millionaire* covers it all in a comprehensive and exciting way. Robb Crocker has created an important resource for videographers—this is a must-read for people who are already involved or new to the stock footage marketplace."

—Tom Spota, Director of Video Acquisition, Shutterstock

"*Stock Footage Millionaire* reaffirms what it has taken me many years to learn. It is brilliantly structured, leaves no stone unturned, and offers the detailed workings of one of the world's most successful video contributors. When followed correctly, it really can make you a stock footage fortune."

—David Baumber (aka Multifocus), Director, Wailing Banshee Ltd.

"It's a rare opportunity to get a complete and organized brain-dump from someone currently operating at the peak of his industry. Robb Crocker takes his years of success and lays it out for you in detail, focusing on a serious and lucrative scale of production."

—Lee Torrens, microstockdiaries.com

"About 8 years ago I started selling my time-lapse videos online and was instantly hooked. I soon realized that this hobby could actually turn into a business. I started to research and read everything I could find relating to stock footage production—to my surprise there was virtually nothing out there written on the subject. For years I stumbled along with rejections and re-shoots, learning from lots of trial and error. Robb's book *Stock Footage Millionaire* finally takes the guesswork out of shooting stock footage, Robb has taken his years of experience and compiled it clearly in his book. Whether you are just starting out in stock footage or are a full time shooter, *Stock Footage Millionaire* is a must read!"

—Daniel Hurst, VIA Films

"If you're a still photographer considering video production, read this book. If you're videographer and want to grow your revenue and profits, read this book. Robb explores in detail everything involved in successful stock video production. He emphasizes the importance of careful preproduction planning for any videographer who hopes to consistently produce salable video clips. Full-time stock video production is not easy. It is about figuring out what will be in demand and producing it efficiently. *Stock Footage Millionaire* will give you the tools you need to be an efficient producer, or help you decide if producing stock video is for you."

—Jim Pickerell, Editor, Selling-Stock.com

STOCK FOOTAGE

Jon —

MILLIONAIRE

Thanks for making Dreams come True!

ROBB CROCKER

STOCK FOOTAGE

$

MILLIONAIRE

THE COMPLETE INSIDERS'
GUIDE TO PRODUCING
STOCK FOOTAGE FOR FUN
AND FORTUNE

TRUNE
PUBLISHING

Published by Trune Publishing, 712 Main Street, Oregon City, OR 97045

Copyright © 2014 by Robb Crocker

All rights reserved.
No part of this book may be reproduced, scanned, or distributed in any printed or electronic from without written permission from the copyright holder or a stated representative.

Cover design by vlados 1 99designs.com
Book design by Draft Lab
Images Courtesy of Robb Crocker, Uberstock, Funnelbox, John Neff, Keith Jefferies, David Baumber, and Shutterstock.

ISBN: 978-0-9906440-0-2

Printed in the United States of America

Table of Contents

Introduction 1

1. The Stock Footage Revolution, "Microstock 2.0" 3

2. How YOU Will Profit in the Microstock Footage Market 15

3. The Big Picture 21

4. Research the Market and Get Rich in a Niche! 27

5. Choosing Your Equipment 47

6. Finding, Casting, and Directing Talent 79

7. Stock Footage Production Process Overview 97

8. Sharpen the Axe (Preproduction) 105

9. The Shoot: Follow the Plan, but Be Ready to Adapt 127

10. Shooting With Purpose 131

11. Taking Care of Business 161

12. Master Your Post 165

13. Finishing Strong 181

14. Optimizing Your Returns 195

15. Keep it Going 201

Acknowledgements 203

About the Author 207

Introduction

I REMEMBER THE MORNING OF April 29, 2007, like it was yesterday. I rolled out of bed, grabbed a cup of coffee and logged in to my microstock footage contributor account to look at my portfolio. And there it was, four footage sales and a balance in my account of $58.90. My face lit up as the thought hit me with crystal clear gravity. I just made nearly $60 while I slept. And not only while I slept, but also on the night of my thirty-third birthday. To top it all off, it was made while I slept, on my birthday, while on vacation in California. Unbelievable, I thought. This is AWESOME!

It wasn't but a few weeks earlier that I decided, on a whim, to upload some footage to iStockphoto.com as a video contributor. I didn't know what to expect . . . but figured I had nothing to lose. Little did I know that just five short years later, that $58 in earnings for the month of April 2007 would turn into over $35,500 in earnings for the month of April 2014.

As I write this book, Uberstock, the company I run that produces stock footage for multiple agency websites, has generated nearly $7,000,000 in sales and has garnered our company over $2,700,000 in royalties. It hasn't been easy. But through hard work, patience, practice and a little luck, I have become a Stock Footage Millionaire.

ONE

The Stock Footage Revolution: "Microstock 2.0"

MOVING IMAGES ARE EVERYWHERE. Traditional static signage and outdoor advertisements are rapidly being replaced with large screens displaying moving images. Automatic tellers and vending machines have simple button- or text-based user interfaces replaced by full-color touch screens. Cell phone displays now typically cover the whole front of the device. The emergence of the mobile Internet has transformed units into mobile multimedia devices capable of showing live broadcast or video on demand. There are already people broadcasting news live from cell phones. It's abundantly clear—the use and demand for moving image content is absolutely exploding.

Along with this explosion in screens, comes an explosion in the need for video content to fill them. And where are many content producers turning to help fill this demand? Microstock footage.

STOCK FOOTAGE 101

Let's first take a step back. TV shows, music videos, web videos and feature films are created by editing together clips of footage. Most often, the producer who is making the video captures that footage. Sometimes, however, they don't have the time or resources to get the footage that they need for their production. If a producer is making a documentary or a commercial film and needs, say, an establishing helicopter aerial of downtown Los Angeles, it can be prohibitively expensive to rent a helicopter, camera, and crew to shoot this. By buying this footage from a stock footage library, that producer can save a great deal of time and money and increase the production value of the finished video. As production budgets are diminished around the world, the need for compelling stock footage is becoming more and more pronounced.

The best way to think about stock footage and its rapid growth in the last five to seven years is that it is the second wave of the microstock revolution—essentially, microstock 2.0. In many ways, the phenomenal growth of stock footage libraries around the world is a natural progression that initially came from the world of still photographs. By now, you are undoubtedly aware of what has happened in the stock *photo* industry. It has been well chronicled how the major stock houses have been transformed by the Internet. Still cameras get better and better, while their cost drops increasingly lower. Desktop editing software is more powerful than ever, and the cost of that power is but a fraction of what it was just a few short years ago. More and more people with access to these lower-priced professional tools are jumping in to the microstock photo arena, and some are making a good living shooting stock photos as their full-time job.

> THE SAME DYNAMICS THAT HOLD TRUE IN THE STOCK PHOTO MARKET *ALSO* HOLD TRUE IN STOCK FOOTAGE.

The same dynamics that hold true in the stock photo market ALSO hold true in stock footage. The same market forces, the same evolution in technology and the same need that have given rise to iStockphoto.com, Shutterstock.com, and Pond5.com have also given dramatic rise to stock footage availability. The microstock *footage* market trajectory is closely mimicking the microstock *photo* market, albeit a few years behind.

Selling stock material is no new business, but the Web 2.0/3.0 eras have changed the distribution and sales process. The transition from only a few large broadcast companies and movie producers to the current situation, where anybody can start a TV channel, totally changes the market for stock footage and ready-made shows. Many of the situations where producers, editors and designers used to have a need for a still image, now require a moving image to make a meaningful impact. And this phenomenon is still in its infancy — as you can see in the still-small number of footage files compared to photos at all of the microstock agencies that sell both photos and footage.

STATS IN THE MICROSTOCK INDUSTRY

- 237 image suppliers reported an aggregate stock of 362 million images worldwide. (GSI Market, Global Survey 2012)
- Shutterstock adds tens of thousands of images each week and currently has more than 35 million images available, with a growing community of over 55,000 contributors. (Shutterstock, April 2014)
- On Shutterstock, nearly 1 million active customers license and download high-quality photos, vectors and illustrations at a rate of more than three image licenses per second. (Shutterstock, April 2014)
- iStockphoto has a catalog fast approaching 10 million files, over 7 million members and pays out approximately $1.9 million per week in artist royalties. (iStockphoto, April 2014)

> - The stock video catalogue that Pond5 has developed now stands at over 2.6 million video clips and is growing by over 100,000 clips every month.
> - TRUE stock photo stars have emerged — Andres Rodriguez, Yuri Arcurs, Kelly Cline and others regularly make several hundred thousand dollars (and more) in sales each year. These stock photo stars have a large following, large studios and staff to help them shoot, edit and upload images.

This book will serve as an important resource as you seek to make money in the exciting new arena of microstock footage. But first, let me lay out the case for microstock footage and why it is such an increasingly demanded visual medium.

Stock footage is an extension and natural outcropping of the still image revolution COMBINED with a rapid change in technology in the world around us. The footage revolution — unlike the stills revolution before it — is more lucrative and growing faster thanks to increasing bandwidth and the increasing need for moving images, not just still images.

I'd like to tell you just how massive this market is, but there is very little financial data available, especially in the microstock footage market where we sell the vast majority of our content. The last publicly available data that I could find is from a 2011 report by the Association of Commercial Stock Image Licensors. ACSIL surveyed 73 of the 300-plus known stock footage companies to generate their findings. In it, the group estimated the stock footage market to be worth just under $400 million per year.

> *Based on the performance of the 73 companies in our sample group, which we believe to be representative of the industry at large… total industry revenue has increased since*

2007 and is now estimated at $394 million per annum. (AC-SIL/Thriving Archives, March 2011)

And in an August 2009 report from the Newsplayer Group PLC, we see that the market was estimated to be growing at 20% per year.

We estimate the stock footage market is growing at more than 20% per annum, fuelled by increased demands for new programming and the huge saving it represents compared with shooting new footage. Interactive technology and the Internet will further contribute to the growth of the market as it makes stock footage cheaper and easier to locate and license. (Newsplayer Group PLC, August 2009)

If I'm to extrapolate these two specific pieces of data, along with what I know from other, not so public sources, I would say that the current stock footage market (as of 2014) is probably sitting somewhere between $600 million and $800 million per year. (This estimate is somewhat confirmed by a Wall Street industry analyst from Wunderlich Securities, who in May of 2014, estimated the annual footage market at between $500 million and $1 billion.)

In layman's terms, that means there is nearly $2 million in stock footage sold each and every day. And if the average clip sells for $200 (some sell for thousands, others for as little as $5), a piece of stock footage is sold every nine seconds, twenty-four hours a day, 365 days a year.

Needless to say, this industry is not only huge, but it's poised for massive growth in both the near and longer term. Finally, it's worth pointing out that almost all microstock footage libraries are less than a decade old. It's still early in the game and, though libraries are continu-

> THIS INDUSTRY IS NOT ONLY HUGE, BUT IT'S POISED FOR MASSIVE GROWTH IN BOTH THE NEAR AND LONGER TERM

ally growing, we are a long way from saturating this market. There is just simply more demand than supply at this point.

A MARKET BEING MET

So who is jumping into this new, exciting industry? A whole range of contributors are filling the need for footage in this new market. In my experience, however, there are five types of contributors that I see with regularity. That's not to say that there aren't other groups that I'm missing. *Stock Footage Millionaire* is written with these contributors in mind:

WHO'S MAKING MONEY SHOOTING STOCK FOOTAGE?

Stock Photographers

As the market for stock photos gets more and more saturated and the price points continue to drop, many stock photographers are moving over to video for the higher price points and artistic challenge that video provides. However, many of them are finding that producing a meaningful, well-lit, well-composed 20-plus-second video clip is exponentially more difficult than snapping a split second in time. Nevertheless, more and more stock photo shooters are adding video to their portfolios. If you are one of those stock photographers, this book will help you make that transition more easily.

Film School Graduates

Film school graduates are graduating into a more uncertain future than many of us have seen in the last two decades. Also, they are coming through school in an environment where they have become accustomed to purchasing stock footage, know the value that stock footage can provide and are looking to join in this exciting movement. These recent graduates aren't even aware of the "old rules" in the stock footage marketplace and are used to grabbing clips for websites, transitional shots and other assignments.

Hobbyists

With the dramatic lowering of prices in cameras, desktop editing software and growing popularity of stock photography sites, we are seeing more and more hobbyists who are looking to move into this arena. Stock footage can be done on your own pace and in your own time without any customers or clients to respond to and deadlines to meet—this is an occupation that can easily be completed in the weekend or after hours or even over a vacation. Both retired and non-retired hobbyists are generating extra income by selling their stock videos. Several prominent contributors have full-time jobs but can also generate substantial income from their other hobby.

> STOCK FOOTAGE CAN BE DONE ON YOUR OWN PACE AND IN YOUR OWN TIME WITHOUT ANY CUSTOMERS OR CLIENTS TO RESPOND TO

Freelance Producers, Editors and Cinematographers

Professionals who already know how to produce great looking content are starting to see microstock footage production as a way to supplement and sometimes even *replace* their primary income. The message boards on all of the large microstock footage websites are filled with stories about video professionals who have quit doing work for hire so they can focus solely on producing a recurring revenue stream through microstock footage sales.

Production Companies

Production companies with excess capacity are starting to turn those idle periods into revenue-generating opportunities. They already have the equipment, people, and know-how to produce professional footage, and they are doing so as a way to help generate a consistent stream of cash flow. For these companies, producing stock footage gives their artists and producers a welcome break from doing client-driven work to create work that is not only fun, but is also free of any client constraints.

Whatever group you find yourself associating with, I hope to provide you with insights, instructions and tips on how to make your stock footage production efforts as fruitful as possible.

WHICH MICROSTOCK AGENCY?

I'm not in the position to recommend any one particular agency. That said, it's important that no matter which agency YOU decide to contribute to, you carefully consider the following questions as you determine which stock agency—or agencies—to partner with:

- What amount of traffic does the site receive?
- How long has the agency been in business?
- What is the pricing structure?
- What percentage of the sale do YOU keep?
- What about exclusivity? Does the agency make you commit to selling content only on their site? If so, does the royalty rate and additional sales make it worthwhile for you to do so?

- How easy is it to upload, keyword, and market your content on their site?
- Does the site have a healthy, helpful community of contributors?
- How long does it take for footage to show up on the site after it has been uploaded?
- How responsive is technical support?
- Who pays if footage is returned?

What makes you so special?

Before I close out this first chapter, I want to answer one lingering question you may have on your mind: Why should you read this information from me? What are my credentials for being in any position to write the book on how to produce microstock footage? I'm glad you asked…

There are dozens of fantastic books available that explain in wonderful detail how to shoot great photos and video. There are a handful that cover stock photography production, and a couple (at the time of this writing) that cover in detail the new and emerging world of microstock footage production. While there are resources that outline the technical aspects of how to upload and market your footage, I haven't been able to find one, as of this writing, that gives a reader the inside scoop of how to actually go about producing footage that is *guaranteed* to sell.

I signed up for my first microstock footage contributor account in March of 2007—and the results have been astounding. I went from making $56.80 in April of 2007 to making over $40,000 a month in peak months.. I began making $1,000 A DAY (on average) in 2011. At the time of this writing, the footage that I've produced has generated over $7 MILLION in revenue through such websites as Shutterstock.com, iStockphoto.com, Gettyimages.com and Pond5.com, to over 30,000 customers around the world. The buyers of my footage come from six continents and they have used my footage in Hollywood film trailers including *The Muppet Movie*; national TV commercials for Intel, Scion, Discover Card, Verizon, and AT&T; award-winning documentaries such as *Food Inc.*; television shows including *Parenthood*, *The Office*, and *The View*; marketing videos for 3M, T-Mobile, Delta Airlines, HP, Wells Fargo, Bank of America, Nike, Motorola, Toshiba, Kodak, and Verizon; US presidential campaign videos for both republicans and democrats; and have even been used for digital display advertising at the top of Times Square.

© Robb Crocker

Stock footage of my daughter, in 2011, displayed on the top screen of Times Square in New York.

My monthly earnings and revenue per image (RPI) stats place me in the top 1% of ALL microstock video shooters, worldwide:

- We regularly sell 150 to 200 video files every week, 52 weeks a year
- Our average revenue per download is $43.65
- I regularly make $10,000 a month while I sleep. That's right. I just wrapped up a $38,500 month in stock footage — I estimate that I made roughly 25% of that money literally while I slept!

There is an old adage that states, "Timing is everything." As far as my success in stock footage goes, I couldn't agree more. Much like stock footage superstars SimonKR, MorganL, Rebelz, Spotmatik, Wavebreak Media, Multifocus, EyeIdea, and a handful of others, I was extraordinarily lucky to have jumped into the microstock footage market when I did; Just as the wave was beginning to form. That timing has proven to be unbelievably advantageous. Hard work, determination, and a bit of talent have all played important roles in my continued success in microstock footage production. But it's also no secret that, quite simply, I was fortunate to start when I did. It was MUCH easier to build a portfolio and garner sales in the infancy of the microstock footage industry. That early success and those corresponding earnings not only helped me to learn how to produce better footage, but also provided the money needed to reinvest in producing more and better footage. No doubt, there is money to be made in stock footage production. But it's also clear that doing so isn't as easy as it used to be.

It's important to recognize that there are a number of different ways in which an artist and/or producer can create footage to sell in the microstock market. Time-lapse videos, 2D and 3D animations, and footage captured with high-speed or other specialized cameras all sell on microstock footage websites. And while most of the concepts and strategies discussed in this book will apply to these production techniques as well, *Stock Footage Millionaire* will focus predominantly on what I view as the most complex type of stock footage production: shooting with talent. I won't spend time diving into the details of setting up a DSLR for shooting time-lapse videos. Nor will I spend any time discussing animation software or techniques. Shooting stock with talent provides a unique set of challenges that aren't inherent in other forms of footage production. It's not to say that other forms aren't equally difficult, they are all just slightly different. And because what I know best is how to shoot with talent, shooting with talent is what I will focus on teaching. Regardless of what technique you use in the production of your footage, I trust that you'll find immense value in both the thinking and strategy, as well as the production, management, and marketing techniques that I'll be sharing with you.

TWO

How YOU Will Profit in the Microstock Footage Market

I HAVE TALKED ABOUT THE explosion in stock footage, in the growing demand of high-quality stock footage and the terrific financial returns that are available in this field. However, I want to be entirely clear that the return you can expect to generate (in terms of both financial gain and artistic satisfaction) is entirely commensurate with the time and effort that you put in. My intent is NOT to gloss over the hard work that is required to build a respectable, money-making stock footage library. But to show you that by working SMARTER while producing stock, you can enjoy greater success quicker when you use the information that I've already learned, tested, and continue to refine.

It's also important to know that, while many of the fundamental concepts, strategies, and practices I'm sharing with you work today, it doesn't necessarily mean they will work tomorrow. Like anything in life, to become one of the best in the world at anything, be it engineering, basketball, teaching, writing, or shooting stock footage, you have to continuously be learning. With this in mind, I want to encourage you to take what I'm teaching you in *Stock Footage Millionaire*, put it to practice, then learn from your efforts and make adjustments as necessary.

THE ROI OF STOCK FOOTAGE

In the early days of microstock footage (like the early days of stock photography) it was literally as simple as setting up a tripod in your backyard and filming everyday scenes with little to no regard for lighting, composition, talent, or direction. Those days are gone. Producers who know HOW to shoot, WHAT to shoot, and WHEN to shoot it will reap the bulk of the microstock footage rewards that continue to grow with each passing day. There is no longer easy money to be made in "lazy production."

> THERE IS NO LONGER EASY MONEY TO BE MADE IN "LAZY PRODUCTION."

In microstock 2.0, shooting uninspired, poorly lit, easily repeatable video will most likely prove to be an unprofitable and completely futile waste of time, money, and resources. The real winners in microstock video 2.0 will be those who work smarter, not harder.

To succeed in microstock video, you'll need to not only research the market, choose a niche, carefully plan your shoots, and take pride and care in producing great looking footage, but you'll also have to make a commitment to carefully investing time, resources, and money to ensure that the rewards you reap will be well worth the investments you make.

It's important to take the long view when it comes to measuring your financial return on stock footage. Earlier, I mentioned both the strong demand for content and the increasing number of contributors that are entering the stock footage market. While there IS a declining return on individual clips over time, I still regularly sell footage that has been on the market for over five years.

The following bell curve illustrates the earning power of clips that are sold through a stock footage agency. As you can see in the curve, the *second* full year of a clip's life is generally its strongest earner. And while it still generates revenue for years after reaching its peak, the rate at which it sells drops pretty significantly after year two, until it reaches a "long tail" period of slow, steady decline in revenue generation for years to come. To reiterate, this curve represents the aggregate average of many clips. Your *actual* earnings from any one clip may vary greatly. In general, we feel that if we are able to recoup our financial investment in a shoot within 12 months, we will be in good shape to actually make a profit on the shoot over years two through five and hopefully beyond.

AVERAGE DOWNLOADS

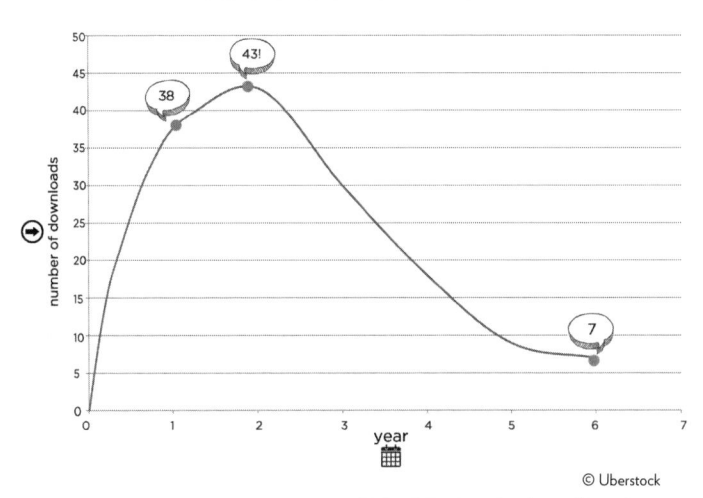

© Uberstock

The graph represents the AVERAGE download profile of an individual clip that sells more than 10 times. Keep in mind, that MOST clips never sell more than 10 times. Almost half of our portfolio has never sold at all.

WHO DO YOU WANT TO BE?

You'll also need to take some time and decide what kind of stock footage producer you want to be. In my opinion, there are three different routes to success in stock footage production.

> **THE THREE ROUTES TO STOCK FOOTAGE SUCCESS**
>
> 1. Lean and Mean. Keep your costs low and your net profit percentage high.
> 2. Calculated Gambles. Find a rich niche with a high barrier to entry and "Bet Big!"
> 3. In Between. Invest modestly to produce high-quality footage in niches that you have experience and confidence in.

Route #1: Lean and Mean

Producers who choose this route keep their expenses low so that most of their income from sales drops straight to the bottom line... and into their pocket. They shoot close to home. They shoot people or things that they have easy access to. They shoot while traveling on vacation or during holidays. They use family and friends for talent and pay them with "thanks" or maybe a meal. They probably shoot by themselves, or maybe ask a friend or family member for help. Again, for the "Lean and Mean" producer, the goal is to keep expenses low and profits high. It's a relatively safe strategy that will produce steady income and can sometimes even generate significant income if a producer has access to particularly good talent and locations. That said, you'll be hard pressed to become a stock footage MILLIONAIRE if your focus is on minimizing expenses rather than maximizing sales.

Route #2: Calculated Gamble

Producers who choose this route look for an underserved niche with a high barrier to entry and spend big to produce footage that very few can, or are willing to shoot. They rent or buy specialized cameras, or camera equipment like high-speed cameras, camera cranes, dollies, or camera stabilization gear. They hire specialized vehicles or rigs such as helicopters or process trailers. Or they spend big on talent ... either by hiring specialized talent for a shoot, like a chimpanzee, or they hire a LOT of talent for a single shoot, like we've done by hiring three entire football teams. Producers who take the calculated gamble approach plan on investing a lot of money to acquire and produce footage, but also plan on MAKING a lot of money with big sales. This is a much riskier strategy probably best left to those who can afford to lose significant money on a shoot or two; much like I have, shooting a highly stylized American football series (to the tune of nearly $20,000). That said, it can also be extremely lucrative, as it has been for my friends at MorganL when they invested heavily into a high-speed "Phantom" Camera package in 2010.

> IT CAN ALSO BE EXTREMELY LUCRATIVE

Route #3: Somewhere In Between

The majority of stock footage producers fall in the "lean and mean" category. After some modest success, however, I encourage those producers to start investing more in their shoots. It can be as simple as hiring additional professional production crew to help you light your scenes better, or hiring professional talent, rather than using good old uncle Charlie... for the thirteenth time. Once you get the hang of how to shoot and get a good idea of what sells well, it's a lot easier to make an investment in shooting high-quality footage that is in limited supply and high demand.

WHERE DOES UBERSTOCK FIT?

Many of my top-selling clips were shot with virtually no cash outlay, using friends and family for talent, shooting in areas that require no location fees, and using only props that I already owned or could easily borrow. The *majority* of my shoots, however, have involved a moderately significant investment of money. In my first few years, my budget for a stock shoot probably averaged $1,000 to $1,500. Now, I probably average closer to $3,000 per shoot. I like to make calculated investments and feel like the return I get by spending this money justifies the risk I take when doing so. The bulk of this money is spent on talent and production crew, as that is where I feel I get the biggest bang for my buck.

> IN MY FIRST FEW YEARS, MY BUDGET FOR A STOCK SHOOT PROBABLY AVERAGED $1,000 TO $1,500.

Over time, my personal success in the stock footage market created the opportunity to grow what started as a side gig into what is now a small business in and of itself. I made the decision fairly early on to invest in employing a small team of full-time staffers, which eventually grew into what Uberstock is today. You'll notice that throughout the book I use a combination of both "I" and "we." This is because I speak from a place of both personal experience, as well as on behalf of my amazing Uberstock team.

THREE

The Big Picture

THERE ARE A NUMBER OF thoughts to keep in mind as you take the steps towards becoming a world-class microstock video producer. While I will be walking you through these steps in further detail throughout the book, I'd like to provide a brief overview of the important topics I will be covering. To become a successful microstock video producer, you will need to have a solid understanding of:

- The buyers of microstock footage and what they are looking for
- Choosing and using video production equipment, including cameras, lights, stands, and specialized equipment like jibs, dollies and more
- How to recruit, hire and direct talent
- How to "sharpen the axe" in preproduction for shooting success
- How to maximize your time, talent and resources during your shoots

- Choosing and using video postproduction equipment and software
- Uploading and keywording your footage
- Marketing your portfolio
- The "co-ompetition" (other stock footage producers who both support AND compete with you)

THE MICROSTOCK VIDEO MARKET: SHOOT WHAT'S NEEDED

It's really as simple as that. Microstock video, like any other product, sells or "sits" based on the laws of supply and demand. If you can find a niche market with no supply and huge demand, your chances of success are multiplied many times over. Finding these niches takes some effort, but when it comes to producing profitable microstock footage, that effort is ALWAYS worth the reward. I'll show you how to find those profitable niches.

CHOOSING AND USING YOUR PRODUCTION EQUIPMENT

You certainly don't need the most expensive camera, lights, and other production equipment, but you should be wise in choosing your production tools before you start down the microstock video path. I'll talk about the most important features to look for in your equipment. But, even more importantly, I'll show you how to get the most out of the equipment you have. Because in the end, it's not the equipment that matters, but what you do with it that counts.

TALENT

When shooting footage involving people, having good talent and, more importantly, knowing how to *direct* that talent will absolutely determine its success or failure. While you don't need to pay top money for talent, you will need attractive, believable subjects to populate your footage. And you will need to know how to direct that talent to ensure you get the best performance possible. A well-composed, well lit, well conceived shot won't sell a LICK if the talent sucks. I'll teach you how to make sure yours doesn't.

"SHARPENING THE AXE" IN PREPRODUCTION

Abraham Lincoln once said that if he had six hours to chop down a tree, he'd spend the first four sharpening the axe. That, my friends, is preproduction. It's not just important. It's critical to your initial and continued success in stock footage production. I'll teach you all of the important details successful stock footage producers get in order *before* they shoot a single frame of footage.

GETTING THE MOST FROM YOUR SHOOT

It's critically important to understand how to maximize your time, talent and resources during your shoot. You want to get as much great footage as possible, in the most efficient way you can. I'll give you tips, tricks and strategies that will show you how to do just that, regardless of whether you're shooting on location or on a stage.

Choosing and Using Your Postproduction Equipment

Again, there are dozens of great software packages available for you to use when it comes to editing and processing your stock footage. And while I won't tell you what specific software to buy or use, I will talk about what you'll need it to do and how to use it most effectively to make sure you're getting the highest quality, most marketable footage possible.

Video Uploading & Keywording

These two steps might seem quite simple, but they are extremely crucial to the success or failure of your stock footage endeavor. Proper keywording in particular is a crucial step in ensuring buyers will find and ultimately purchase your clips. I'll show you best practices in keywording, learned from years of trial and error experience, as well as in-depth research.

MARKETING YOUR PORTFOLIO

Having a portfolio of great-looking clips is important, but if people can't find them, it's nearly useless. I'll show you how to get needed exposure to your footage both on the stock footage marketplace websites, as well as outside of those websites to help drive demand and sales.

IS IT WORTH IT?

After reviewing the list above and considering all that may be required, do you feel that it is still a lucrative enough field to enter? Is it worth your time and attention to purchase or rent (or otherwise acquire) the camera, software, models and lighting equipment that may be required? Based on over seven years of experience and my own humble beginnings in microstock footage - my answer is an unequivocal *"YES"!* There are few mediums that are growing as fast as stock video and few equivalent opportunities to generate significant revenue shooting for yourself on your own schedule.

FOUR

Research the Market and Get Rich in a Niche!

DANIEL HURST AND LUKE MILLER, known as "MorganL" to the microstock world, didn't know exactly how things would pan out before purchasing their $100,000 Phantom HD Gold camera package. Although they knew there was virtually NO ultra-high-speed content available in the microstock footage market, they also didn't know for sure if there was an actually market for the footage they would be able to produce with this new camera. Ultimately, they decided that the potential rewards outweighed the financial risk. They took the plunge, bought the camera and the rest is history. Once they mastered this new tool and focused their efforts on shooting content in high demand, they very nearly owned that high-speed niche for a number of years. They enjoyed tremendous sales that generated more than enough money to cover the cost of the equipment. Because of their ability to see an unserved niche in the library, and their bravery to bet big on the equipment they needed to produce that footage, Daniel and Luke saw returns that not only paid off financially, but also made them superstars in the microstock footage industry.

Now, while you may not have the resources, or the confidence to bet big like MorganL, you certainly *can* find an unserved or underserved niche in the stock footage market. Although it is getting harder and harder to find these niches, there are still plenty of them out there. If you want to experience significant success in stock footage, it would behoove you to find one of these niches of your own . To succeed in this endeavor, you need to either predict the future or create your own niche.

Let's talk first about predicting the future.

ROBB'S RULES

TWO WAYS TO CAPITALIZE ON A NICHE:

1. Predict the future and determine what you think buyers will want more of
2. Create a niche based on your experience, talents, or available resources

---

"SKATE TO WHERE THE PUCK WILL BE"

It's important not only to know what buyers are looking for and buying TODAY, but also to have a good idea of what buyers will be looking for and buying three months to a year from now. Wayne Gretzky, arguably the greatest hockey player to ever live, said he never skated to the hockey puck; he skated to where he felt the puck was going to be. If you want to make money as a stock footage producer, you can't think about following the herd, you need to think about blazing a trail. You need to take a macro view of the world around you and look for clues as to what stock footage buyers will be looking for in the future. That future can be both near-term and long-term. For instance, we all know that in the United States, the baby boomer population is aging quickly. And with an aging population comes many interesting topics that will be talked about and covered in the media, healthcare and retirement being at the top of that list. When the iPad came out in 2009, an astute producer could have quickly bought the first model and shot all kinds of footage with all kinds of different people using it. In addition to experiencing a significant head start in providing that footage to buyers, more than likely, they also would have seen a significant return on that effort.

> IF YOU WANT TO MAKE MONEY AS A STOCK FOOTAGE PRODUCER, YOU CAN'T THINK ABOUT FOLLOWING THE HERD.

TAKE STOCK OF YOUR RESOURCES

Another, and I would argue better, way to seek a niche is to look at the resources you have currently available to you and exploit the heck out of them. As far as resources go, you need look no further than at the people, places, and things you have easy access to.

It's no secret that I have three beautiful young daughters (I'm slightly biased, of course) who are all growing up both in front of and around the camera. I make a very deliberate effort to restrict the amount of footage I shoot of them for fear of burning them out or giving them reason to resent the camera and me. That said, I do shoot them on a fairly regular basis, at least four of five times a year. And, more often than not, these shoots generate great footage that sells.

John Neff, a successful stock footage producer from South Carolina, worked for over a decade as a Radiology Technologist in hospitals and other medical facilities, before starting his stock footage career. Having access to these facilities gave John a HUGE advantage when it came to shooting medical footage. As a matter of fact, John has an astonishing library of over 1,100 medical-related clips, most of which originated as a result of his experience in, and access to, the medical facility where he worked. And that footage has sold well. So well, in fact, that when John's job was eliminated at the radiology department, he didn't go out to look for a new one. He turned to producing stock footage full time and makes more now than he did while working for someone else.

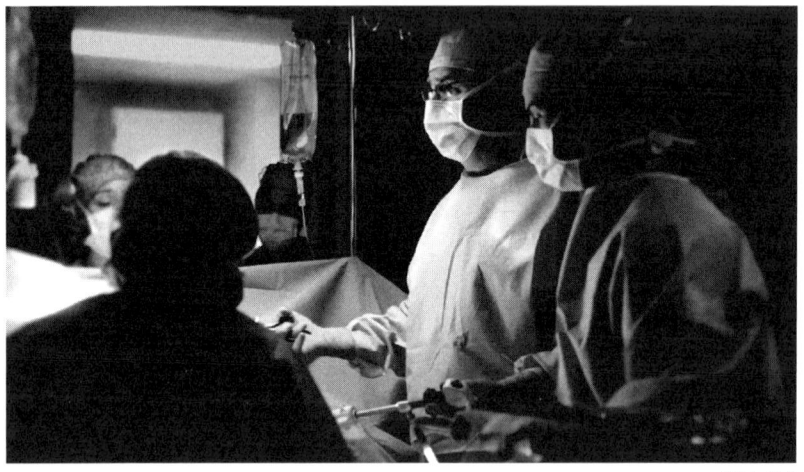

© John Neff

Having access to a medical facility has proven to be a huge differentiator for John Neff.

PLAY TO YOUR STRENGTHS

Another great way to produce footage that sells is to leverage your talents and experience. For instance, if you grew up on a farm and have been riding horses since you were three years old, who better to shoot horseback riding, or the care and feeding of horses than you? True, the market for horseback riding footage may not be nearly as big as other markets, but that's okay. Your footage will probably be some of the best, most authentic footage available, which should (as long as it's shot well) attract the majority of buyers looking for that type of content. On the other hand, if you were to chase a niche which you have NO experience or knowledge in, the odds of your footage looking authentic enough to be a top seller would be slim, regardless of how well it was shot. If you are a really good tennis player, producing authentic, believable tennis footage should be easy for you. If you're a great cook, shoot cooking footage. A fantastic welder produces extraordinary welding footage.

FIND A NICHE THAT YOU ALREADY KNOW SOMETHING ABOUT

One of the ways I learned this firsthand was in the production of golf stock footage. I've played golf since the age of 11. I know what is believable and what isn't. Because I have played so long and have taken plenty of lessons, I also have a classic-looking golf swing. So when I wanted to shoot golf stock footage, it was relatively easy for me to do so. Not only did I know what to look for, but I also served as talent for many of the shots.

If you can find a niche that you already know something about, you will be ahead of the game.

A silhouette of my swing in one of our most popular golf clips.

SEARCHING FOR GOLDMINES

As with any free-market activity, supply and demand ultimately determines how successful a business endeavor will be. Find a market with huge demand and little supply and you've found yourself a microstock footage goldmine.

Regardless as to whether you are going to seek a niche based on your experience and available resources, or one based on what you believe is a future trending need, a great place to begin is by researching what's happening in current pop culture. TV commercials. Magazines. Websites. News. Study it all and make an educated guess on what people are looking for, then look to see if it's available on the microstock footage website(s) you sell through. If it isn't, you have found a potential niche. As soon as you find what you think might be a potential niche, take the next step and think about who your potential customer would be in this niche. Get specific—ad agency, political campaign manager, church, college, etc. If you can get a sense of who would potentially buy footage in this niche, you can tailor HOW you shoot the footage to make sure it's most appealing to those buyers.

NATURE ABHORS A VOID…. AND SO DOES THE MICROSTOCK FOOTAGE MARKET

As soon as you find that profitable niche, exploit it to the fullest, for as long as you profitably can. But ALWAYS keep your eyes peeled for that NEXT profitable niche. Once you start selling lots of footage in a particular niche, it WILL raise the eyebrows of other microstock footage producers. Many of these producers will want to join to party. It's an inevitable part of the game. If you find a truly unique niche, however, it really isn't that problematic. In many markets, and especially in microstock video, there is a first mover advantage. Since you will have uncovered the niche and attacked it with dozens or even hundreds of fantastic-looking clips and made hundreds or thousands of sales, it will prove EXTREMELY difficult for any newcomers to break into that niche. Your clips will have gathered so many views and sales, that they will continue to appear at the top of any potential buyer's search results. The only way you can start losing some of your market share in that niche, is if a new producer does something significantly different enough to warrant a potential buyer PASSING on your clips first.

Say, for example, you determine that there is almost NO microstock footage of people playing cricket, a sport you happen to know something about. You know that this sport is extremely popular in certain parts of the world and feel that it would be worth the effort to acquire some cricket footage to sell in your portfolio. You take the time to shoot and produce some great footage, get it uploaded and keyworded, and much to your delight, your cricket footage starts selling like HOTCAKES. As you watch your earnings grow like a well-watered money tree, other microstock video producers start to take notice and they too start shooting and uploading cricket footage to their portfolio. If they simply copy the footage you've shot, they may be able to take a small portion of your sales, but there is little chance that they will take a significant piece of your cricket footage sales pie. An astute producer, however, will study what you've shot and find a new niche in the cricket arena, or a niche within a niche. They may

MAKE SURE YOU FILL AS MANY *PROFITABLE* MICRO-NICHES AS POSSIBLE

see that your cricket footage features only amateurs playing in a local park. If they were to shoot footage of professional cricket players playing in a stadium, they could very well find a hungry market ready to buy this new footage. And they might be able to take a significant portion of your cricket niche sales, even with your first mover advantage. If you're smart, therefore, when you find a profitable niche, make sure you fill as many *profitable* micro-niches as possible. Shoot social AND professional cricket players. Shoot European cricket players and Indian cricket players. Shoot young cricket players and old cricket players. Make sure that if there is a profitable micro-niche within that cricket niche, you've got it covered. (The key phrase here is *profitable*. Shooting Asian cricket players dressed in bunny costumes would be a micro-niche, but it certainly wouldn't be a *profitable* micro-niche to pursue.)

BECOME AN IMAGE COLLECTOR

A trick that I've used the last several years to help direct me in choosing new niche markets to shoot is to maintain a virtual folder of pop culture footage and images, as well as a folder or lightbox of top-selling stock footage. I'd recommend that you do the same to help keep tabs on the ever-evolving footage and imagery space. A file, lightbox or watch list can help in many different ways. You'll use your collection for market research; to identify concepts; to analyze lighting techniques, use of color, gestures, and the integration of the text/copy with the file. Additionally, it's unbelievably helpful to simply browse the Internet for ideas and look for trends.

© Uberstock

With rising social awareness of bullying in schools, I shot a number of clips that involved student bullying and loneliness.

The one thing you can't use your online folder or lightbox for is copying. That is copyright infringement and, very simply, wrong. Even if you make small changes in your version of the footage that you've seen, regardless of whether it's stock footage or otherwise, if it is "substantially similar," you could be held liable. To avoid the dangers of infringement, identify *the idea* behind the video—the concept, the execution, and the lighting technique—and distill the essence down to something YOU can do. What is the director doing that makes it appeal to you on a basic level? If you look at this file, you'll note my attempt at conveying concepts of alienation, loneliness, isolation and rejection. Although I think these issues are conveyed well in this shot of a junior-high student, there are surely an innumerable amount of images and settings to convey these same concepts.

> YOU OWE IT TO YOURSELF TO ENSURE YOU STAY ON TOP OF THE POPULAR STYLES THAT SEEM TO BE EMERGING IN MASS MEDIA

A great benefit of monitoring both the latest in popular media and top-selling stock footage is knowing which clips are in the highest demand. *Despite whether you personally like the clips, remember that there was SOME type of vetting process and this clip was chosen by buyers.* You might not like the latest advertising campaign selling TVs, or furniture, or shampoo, but if there is a consistent theme to all of it—you owe it to yourself to ensure you stay on top of the popular styles that seem to be emerging in mass media.

PERPETUAL NICHES

While finding underserved niches is the optimal way to rack up sales and profits, there are certain markets that are so HUGE and the demand for stock footage so great, that there is always room for new micro-niches.

For instance, business stock footage is a very, very popular market segment—and there is still a great deal of room to grow. Again, look for contemporary themes (teamwork, energy, synergy, etc.). Don't be dismayed by the large number of clips that are already in place on these footage libraries or by the competition—there is still plenty of room for your footage.

There are many LARGE stock footage market segments with an insatiable need for new content. They are wide-reaching segments that need to convey emotional concepts in new and ever-expanding ways through stock footage. So, another way to find a niche is to shoot with specific conceptual content in mind.

THE ABCS OF CONCEPTS

Certain concepts can stretch across various industries and geographies and convey elemental truths (teamwork, love, joy, happiness, freedom) to which a very large segment of stock footage buyers will gravitate. When shooting concepts, one of my fundamental lessons has been to shoot precisely for the middle—in essence, trying to capture underlying and broad elements that are applicable and timeless.

The most successful stock footage is that which conveys an immediate message to the viewer: It will communicate a thought or a concept of universality. If concepts are the ideas or emotions conveyed in a clip, then it is through the use of the talent or subject matter that the idea is conveyed. If you can find the right symbol, you can find the right subject matter… but not always vice versa.

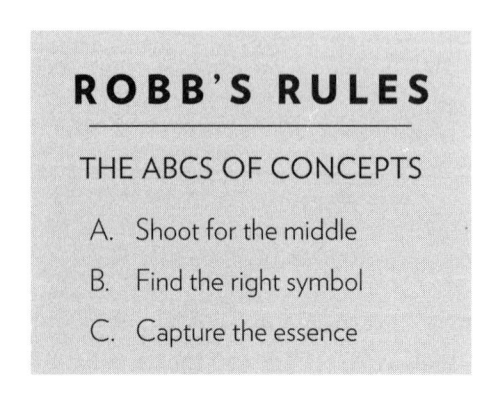

> **ROBB'S RULES**
>
> THE ABCS OF CONCEPTS
>
> A. Shoot for the middle
> B. Find the right symbol
> C. Capture the essence

For example, the concept of winning can be conveyed by a runner breaking the tape at the finish line, a still-life panning shot of a rack of medals, a silhouette of a hand with a trophy raised high, or a simple laurel wreath. I have actually used one of my own clips in my "Dark Fitness" series to convey this same image. It is of a middle-aged man in slow motion doing a fist pump. The excitement and exhilaration on his face is very evident. The subject matter changes, but the icons do not.

Winning!

How well you make use of this information and match your concepts to a symbol can make an important difference in your success in stock—especially in helping you to make significant money in this field. Nailing the essence of a concept or idea can help your footage stand out and buyers will begin to identify your work with high-quality, well-thought-out material.

Zero in on the theme and concept that you are trying to capture, pay close attention to current trends, execute a technically sound shoot, and the rest will take care of itself.

DEVELOP YOUR STYLE

Once you've settled on a concept, next comes style. I'll define style as:

- Your point of view
- The distinctive, characteristic way of seeing that distinguishes your work from others
- Your expression of an idea
- The form, rather than the content of a footage clip.

When it comes to style, HOW you shoot is just as important as WHAT you shoot. And developing your own style is central to success in stock footage. It is important to understand, define, and refine your style and know where it fits in the market. Once you have a clear idea of your style, the next step is to match it with what is useful for stock. Take some time to consider the composition, background, color and talent and use those to express or re-enforce your personal style.

Taking a popular concept—winning, say—then giving it a style that is all yours, that has been tested against the market and against the footage that appears to be doing well is a sure-fire way to profitability. When used properly, this will enhance a clip's salability.

WHAT SELLS?

An example here may be helpful: One of my most successful clips was shot using an early camera with virtually no overhead. The model was my daughter and she was in a grass field right next to our home. The 29-second clip that came out of that quick expedition has generated over $7,000 in royalty earnings to date and it brings out the point I'm trying to illustrate—try to embody concepts and themes. A well-crafted, well-lit video of a young girl in a field with a handful of daisies has sold shampoo, led worshippers in singing at church and introduced fitness products to clients in Atlanta (that one was a head-scratcher). But what's even better is that I asked my wife to join my daughter and shot a few more shots. That extra 30 minutes of shooting generated another handful of clips that, to date, have earned over $8,400 additional royalties.

This shot of my then three-year-old daughter has generated over $7,000 in royalties.

The extra 30 minutes it took to shoot this shot of my daughter with my wife generated an additional $8,400 in royalties.

Look at this image of three girls holding hands walking in a field. This simple concept was able to capture the essence of **youth**, **energy**, **happiness**, **joy**, and **family**. I have made over $8,000 in royalties on this one clip—and I spent probably $30 to produce it. This is a perfect example of how relatively easy and cheap it can be to produce a compelling and profitable clip.

© Uberstock

The ultimate in ROI. One hour of shooting with our friend's three girls resulted in a series of clips that have generated over $10,000 in royalties.

I've learned a great deal about what sells and what doesn't in the world of microstock footage. Not only from my shining successes but also from my miserable failures. And while there have been many ingredients to those various successes, if there is one law I've come to live by, it's the law of supply and demand.

Find a niche with low supply and high demand, and you have a recipe for success.

SQUIRRELS, MISSING TEETH, PLAIN VANILLA, AND LACK OF FOCUS

There are a number of reasons that a particular shoot fails to generate footage that sells. Here are a handful of methods through which I've managed to fall flat on my face.

A good friend and fellow microstock producer, Keith Jefferies, aka Ascalon Films, once told me of the "incredible squirrel footage" he was able to capture fairly early in his microstock production career. The lighting was incredible. The squirrel was cuddly. The compositions were fantastic. The footage looked great. Trouble was, not many people are looking for squirrel footage. Not surprisingly, it didn't sell.

© Keith Jefferies, Ascalon Films

A cute, cuddly squirrel shot by Ascalon Films that doesn't sell.

Yes, I've captured my share of "squirrel footage." (Actually, mine was barn swallows feeding their babies.) The temptation stock shooters have to capture that which is easy to grab, is universal. Almost everyone does it. IF (and that's a big IF) there is significant demand for footage that just happens to be easy for you to capture, then by all means, shoot away. Keep in mind, however, that most footage that

FIND A NICHE WITH LOW SUPPLY AND HIGH DEMAND, AND YOU HAVE A RECIPE FOR SUCCESS.

is easy for you to shoot is probably easy for everyone else to shoot as well. If you want to shoot a squirrel, go ahead. Just know that, while cute, he probably won't help you generate much in the way of sales.

3.

If you're going to shoot footage that involves talent, make sure you are casting good talent. Specifically, whenever possible, hire attractive and believable talent. If you're going to spend time and money shooting footage, you have to make sure you are producing footage worth buying. A huge part of determining whether your footage will be worth buying is predicated on the quality of the talent. I'm tempted to tell you a story about how a model with super attractive photos in her online profile showed up to a studio shoot (with lights, props, and plenty of crew) only to reveal the reason her online photos never showed her teeth. Needless to say, we didn't shoot any footage of her smiling, which, in my opinion, pretty much killed all of the potential sales we could have made with her footage. Remember, all things being equal, footage of attractive people will ALWAYS outsell that of average looking people.

It's not politically correct to say so. It might not even be fair. But, unfortunately, it's the truth. Hire attractive, believable talent. (We'll talk more about this in a later chapter.)

ROBB'S RULES

FOR FOOTAGE THAT SELLS

1. Avoid that easy, tempting "squirrel footage"
2. Footage of attractive people always outsells average looking people
3. Less vanilla = more money
4. Tailor to trends
5. Keep it fresh
6. Go with what you know!

THINK UNIQUE

If you want to shoot footage that rises above the crowd, you should strive to shoot it in a way that is unique. Invest some time into thinking about camera angles, focal lengths, lighting setups, camera movement, and action within the frame (also known as blocking). If you shoot footage that looks average, you'll sell an average amount of footage. (And let me tell you, average stock video producers aren't generating thousands of dollars a month in royalties.) If you want to see numbers with lots of commas in your bank account, stay clear of "vanilla" looking footage.

KEEP UP WITH THE TIMES

Though it is a more sophisticated market than years prior, some aspects of stock footage have not changed: Videographers should still look for universal subjects and concepts, but the look of the images changes with the style of the era and even from season to season. It is no longer easy to generate significant returns shooting stock footage. *It is a very competitive field and mediocre footage won't garner much, if any, MONEY.* It's critical that your clips are as timely and relevant as current trends dictate. Successful footage today sends more than just a clear message—it stands out and effectively communicates concepts directly to viewers. The new world of footage mandates that videographers execute with finesse and meticulous craftsmanship—and often in the most contemporary or compelling new style—influenced by everything from YouTube to the nightly news to the latest brand films from Fortune 500 firms. You should be an avid consumer of the latest trends in advertising in general and moving footage in particular.

> GIVE THE BUYERS THE TIMELY, FRESH, UPDATED, AND TRENDY FOOTAGE THEY NEED

FEED THE BEAST

Because of this breathtaking rush to supply material, all footage libraries are acutely aware of the need for a constant supply of fresh, exciting new footage. In an interesting turn of events, sometimes buyers will shy away from the best, most popular clips simply because they think that everyone else has it, and this isn't just artistic snobbery. ***There is a real concern that using the same clip in one client project will turn off the client to their creativity—after all, do they want the image that's selling shampoo also in a cell phone commercial?*** It falls to all of us to give the buyers the timely, fresh, updated, and trendy footage they need. All stock footage marketplaces actively encourage videographers to produce new footage—in some (very rare) cases, they participate in the process themselves through financial support for footage shooters. In today's competitive arena, all of us must go to the limit to meet market expectations and retain a piece of the financial pie.

Clients are using ALL styles in an effort to break the mold, be fresh and stay relevant. Several years ago, advertising adopted a style of grainy, gritty reality that was previously seen only in photojournalism. ***In general, what emerges first in popular media will eventually move over to stock libraries.*** This is an important point that I should re-emphasize. If you want to see what may be popular stylistically—soft lighting, oblique angles, lens flares, unexpected cropping—look first to popular media. Demand for stock footage with these traits may only be a few months behind.

STAY TRUE TO YOU!

You can research what's current by looking at all kinds of popular media, gleaning which styles are in favor. However, there is no point in trying to shoot in a style that is in vogue if you aren't adept and skilled at emulating it. As important as it is to be aware of market trends and "faddish" swings toward specific styles in media, understanding your own abilities and where they fit within those trends is also extremely important. Express your vision of the current style with panache and your own inspiration:

- Know who you are as a videographer and as an artist
- Have a sense of the trends and shifting markets
- Do what you care about—what you can do wholeheartedly
- Keep what is spontaneous and authentic in your view and style
- Always remember to ask yourself: WILL IT SELL?!

Some videographers are lured by the stories of huge sums to be gathered from certain types of clips. However, shooting a subject matter or in a style that is not natural to you is a sure recipe for failure. You should avoid shooting what doesn't feel right or what doesn't excite or please you artistically—whether you can profit from it or not. *If it's contrary to the way you see the world, to what you care about visually, then it won't work—for you, for the footage library, and certainly, not for the stock footage buyer!*

> SHOOTING A SUBJECT MATTER OR IN A STYLE THAT IS NOT NATURAL TO YOU IS A SURE RECIPE FOR FAILURE

FIVE

Choosing Your Equipment

THERE ARE A HANDFUL OF mission-critical pieces of equipment you will need to shoot great stock footage and a boatload of extras that you could acquire, if your heart so desires. Let's start with the necessities.

THE CAMERA

You could ask ten different stock footage producers which type of camera is best for shooting and you just might get ten different answers. The exact make and model of camera isn't all that important. What IS important is to make sure you're securing a camera that not only shoots great footage but that you can also learn to use well. In general, I'd recommend that you get a camera that shoots the highest resolution footage you can afford. When I started shooting stock footage, some producers were still shooting in standard-definition NTSC or PAL. Most producers knew, however, that HD was the future of all broadcast video and sought to acquire HD-resolution footage. Fast forward a few years, and we see that things have changed again. HD is here, but the future is now "Ultra." 4K Ultra HD, that is.

With this in mind, if at all possible, you should try to shoot in Ultra HD 4K resolution, as this is a somewhat future-proof format. It's not imperative, because the demand for Ultra HD footage (at the time of this writing in 2014) is still very low. That said, in the next decade, Ultra HD will at some point become the standard and most broadcast buyers will want to purchase for that standard. The future of Ultra HD aside, at the very least, you'll need to have a camera that shoots 1080p HD resolution.

In addition to your camera, you should also seriously consider purchasing a professional monitor to use while shooting. Separate monitors make it a ton easier to check and keep focus during your shoots. Especially if you are using a camera with a small LCD screen or with no screen at all. I've ruined plenty of shots because I was viewing a small screen that appeared in-focus out on the shoot. I might be a few dollars richer had I packed a monitor to use instead of trying to wing it with the built-in monitor on the camera.

"STICKS & TOYS"

A tripod, or "sticks" as they are known in the production industry, are an absolute necessity when it comes to shooting stock footage. MOST of the footage you are going to shoot will use a tripod. As such, you DON'T want to scrimp in this department. Get the best tripod you can afford. Professional tripods can run anywhere from $1,000 to $30,000 or more, depending on the brand and model. You certainly don't need to spend $30,000 on a tripod, but you also don't want to think about getting by with a $129 discount-store special. Keep in mind, if you buy a cheap photo tripod, you aren't going to be able to pan and tilt while shooting, which will greatly restrict

> GET THE BEST TRIPOD YOU CAN AFFORD

your ability to make your footage more dynamic than your competition. If you buy a "fluid-head" tripod from a reputable manufacturer like Sachtler, Vinten, O'Connor, Gitzo, or Manfrotto, you should be fine. Make sure it's big enough to adequately carry the load of your particular camera. If you have a large camera, with lots of accessories, you're going to have to pony up for a larger tripod. If you don't want to spend the $500 to $1,500 for a decent fluid-head tripod, you can rent them from a local video production rental facility. In most major cities,

> YOU CAN GET SOME PRETTY COOL SHOTS USING INEXPENSIVE TOYS AND A LITTLE IMAGINATION

you'll be able to find really nice tripods to rent for less than $50 a day. Another option is to look at buying a used professional tripod online. (I've purchased three great tripods on eBay with great success.) Keep in mind, however, if you buy a used tripod that is beaten up, you might have to pay up to have it refurbished. Again, don't skimp on your sticks. A good tripod is an absolute must.

For the more creative and adventurous types, there are plenty of camera goodies to try out too. You can buy dollies, jibs, cranes, camera stabilizers, camera sliders, or any other number of gadgets, widgets and do-dads. If you know how to use some of these fun tools, they can add significant production value to your footage and can help differentiate your content to help increase sales.

If you want to try using some of these fun toys, but don't have the money needed to buy the professional stuff, get creative. You may not have the budget to buy a $50,000 PeeWee dolly, but you can certainly go to Toys 'R' Us and buy a $20 skateboard. With a little practice and patience, you can get some pretty cool shots using inexpensive toys and a little imagination. Do a Google search for DIY camera support, DIY camera dolly, or DIY camera jib, and you'll find all kinds of fun things to try out that can add significant production value to your shoots without costing a ton of money.

Yes, camera goodies can be fun, and they can add production value to your footage. Keep in mind, however, that whenever you add these types of gadgets to the mix, it complicates your shoot, takes additional time to set up, and could take a lot of trial and error before you not only learn how to use it properly, but also might take multiple runs to get even a single shot properly captured on-set.

> ## ROBB'S RULES
>
> ### CAMERA GOODIES
>
> 1. Think twice, if it takes longer than 30 minutes to set up.
> 2. Think twice, if it takes a lot of practice to master and you don't have time to practice.
> 3. If you're not sure about how useful it will be, try renting it for a shoot before you buy it.
> 4. Make sure you have a great fluid-head tripod before you spend significant money on other goodies.
> 5. Before you buy any goodie, make sure you're acquiring it to generate more sales, not to "shoot cool footage."

LIGHTING EQUIPMENT

Owning a package of professional lighting equipment can make an enormous difference in the quality of your footage, especially if you are shooting footage indoors. There are many different types of lights you can acquire and use for your shoots, each with its own pluses and minuses.

If you are new to shooting stock footage and on a limited budget, purchasing lights is not a must. But if that is the case, you should plan on shooting most of your footage where you are able to use direct and reflected natural light, such as outside, or in spaces with lots of large exterior windows. To help reflect light, you should purchase some light-reflecting instruments, like a photoflex or flex-fill reflecting disc. They are light, portable, and made specifically for photographers and videographers. Foam core rigid insulation also makes a great light-reflection device. You can buy this white insulation in different thicknesses at most building supply stores.

If you are able to put together a lighting kit for your shoots, you should think through how you plan on using the kit. Will you be using it to supplement daylight most of the time? If so, you'll want to take that into account when choosing the color temperature of your lights. (We'll talk about color temperature later.) Will you often be travelling long distances? If so, you might want to think about investing in LED technology to help keep the size and weight of the light to a minimum. Are you planning on shooting high-speed footage? If so, you'll need some incredibly powerful, flicker-free light sources. There are a ton of options available as you look at putting together a light kit. Whatever option you decide, make sure it's going to fit the type of shooting you do most and plan on renting additional lights for those shoots you do only on occasion.

TAKE CONTROL

If you listen to the industry experts and regularly read the magazines, blogs, and websites that cater to our industry, you can quickly be dismayed at the price associated with producing footage. You might also feel equally frustrated at the constant need to stay in front of the latest technology.

In this chapter, my intention is not to begin a dialogue on which camera is the best to own, based on pixel rate or model. My goal in this section is to discuss the practical aspects of actually operating whatever camera you choose to purchase and the way to make sure your clips give you the highest possible return—*regardless of the camera that you use*. Also, many features on cameras are simply not helpful or even very useful, and NO feature on a camera will overcome a deficiency in the operator.

> NO FEATURE ON A CAMERA WILL OVERCOME A DEFICIENCY IN THE OPERATOR

A good place to start is to talk about camera automation. Quite simply, don't do it.

The sheer volume of controls available to the operator on even the most basic camera can daunt many first-time stock shooters. However, I strongly recommend NOT allowing the camera to make too many of its own decisions. There are four key options that you should de-automate that immediately come to mind:

Autofocus systems

When you have a simple frame with a static subject, autofocus can serve a useful purpose and generally does a fine job. When shooting stock, however, this "static frame, static subject" element will rarely, if ever come into play. It's also true that you will often frame a subject somewhere OTHER than the middle of the frame, which is where most autofocus systems generally default. Cameras and lenses aren't smart enough to figure out what you are trying to focus on all the time. And they certainly can't ANTICIPATE what you are going to want to focus on next like only you can. That's why YOU need to be the one determining where the camera is focused and both when and how that focus changes.

Autoexposure

Autoexposure systems rely almost exclusively on feedback loops that don't always respond instantaneously or as quickly as you need it to for your clip. For example, a move into a bright situation may start off overexposed and will fade to correct exposure in one, two or even three seconds. Additionally, they often expose for parts of the frame that you don't care about, like an overcast sky, which ruins the exposure you need of your model's face. Learn how to use your camera's over- and underexposure guides and control the exposure yourself.

Auto white-balance controls

These may correct where you aren't looking for a correction. Quite often, you might want to keep the warm color of an interior scene that you've worked hard to create. However, left to its own devices, the camera will attempt to create a balance that neutralizes the atmosphere you've worked so hard to stage. This can be especially frustrating if you have invested money on filters, special lights, or time ensuring that you film at the appropriate time of day for the correct mood. Learn how to properly white-balance your camera, then set it yourself.

Microphones

It isn't often that we record sound with our stock footage. On the occasion that it is warranted, however, it's best to do it right. When you are shooting stock with audio as a vital component, I learned early on that automatic level or gain controls for the built-in microphone work well when there is steady and constant levels of sound that you are looking to record. However, during quiet times, microphones will pick up ALL the background noise—as the gain control will have been automatically raised—and will be distorted when there is a loud sound. It's better to use a field microphone that will help you direct the sound you are looking to capture and not the scatter-shot approach that is, unfortunately, too common in much of the stock footage that is being shot today.

GET TO KNOW YOUR CAMERA

Each camera model has its own peculiarities under various shooting situations. It's vital that you become very familiar with the camera you are either renting or have purchased before locking locations, booking talent and venturing on set. This familiarity should include a complete and thorough understanding of the operation and function of all of the manual controls, buttons, and switches. *You don't want to spend precious on-set time learning or re-learning the basics of camera operation.*

Make sure you not only understand what is in the camera manual, but also what nuances and changes arise when you actually shoot with the camera. There is no substitute for spending a LOT of time in a non-pressure situation becoming familiar with the way your camera performs and operates under different scenarios. The only way to get this experience is to spend quality time with the equipment in a variety of settings. Shoot indoors. Shoot outdoors. Shoot during the day and night. Shoot with different lenses, if they are interchangeable. The best way to get to know your camera is to use it a LOT. So go out and shoot.

Finally, there are many good tutorials for many different cameras. Start at the manufacturer's website, but also do a search for the particular model that you have, as well as basic tutorial sites. YouTube is a fantastic place to search for tutorials and reviews about equipment. Before shooting any footage with a new camera, I would absolutely encourage you to watch some YouTube tutorials and practice on your own.

FINAL SHOOTING TIPS

Over the past 16 years of shooting professionally, I've learned some additional tips and tricks from others as well as from my own experience:

- Whenever possible, rely on a field monitor to check focus.
- Pay attention to the zebra stripes displayed in most cameras when shooting in manual mode. When properly set, they will warn you about overexposed areas.
- Make every effort to start recording BEFORE the action begins. You want to give yourself two to three seconds of lead time before any movement commences in the shot.
- Similarly, stop the recording LATE, only after the action has finalized. I have caught many, many candid and poignant moments that have gone on to become great-selling clips after the official shot was deemed completed.
- If you must shoot handheld, to help steady the image, bring some extra weight to hold down the camera OR lean yourself (as operator) against a structure to provide any stability you can. Unlike photography where you are looking for just one or two great split-seconds, stock videography requires 10-plus seconds of clean, smooth camera operation. Use your environment and keep your breathing slow and steady to keep camera activity to an absolute minimum.

RECORDING GOOD AUDIO

Several stock agencies allow you to upload audio with your video. If you are going to use this approach, ensure that the audio is appropriate to the action in the clip OR eliminate all audio entirely. If there is one common factor that screams poor quality, it's bad audio on your stock clip. No matter how good the story, camerawork, and acting within the clip may be, poor or badly placed audio will not allow the stock buyer to appreciate it. (Interestingly, I have found that well-placed audio can dramatically help sell a clip! Several of my animal, golf, and driving clips, I believe, are actually accentuated by the presence of audio.)

Many stock shooters fail to recognize that sound recording is a very precise art. While the basic concepts are easy to learn, the craft is truly learned over time and while working in a variety of diverse situations.

Although you won't always (or ever) be able to hire a seasoned pro to record sound, try to find the appropriate microphone settings that will make the action in your clip pop and add value to the stock footage buyer.

10 IMPORTANT THINGS TO REMEMBER IF YOU RECORD SOUND:

1. Use the right type of microphone in the right environment. Don't use a shotgun mic in a situation that doesn't warrant its use.
2. Whenever possible, hide the microphone from view so it doesn't call attention to itself.
3. If you are recording dialogue, make sure the person wearing the mic is comfortable with how it's attached.
4. Use a windscreen when recording sound outdoors. Even if you don't have gale force winds, the acoustically transparent covering protects the mic's elements from nature.

5. Record all sound at a decent level; you can always lower the volume in editing.
6. Always record without filters or equalization in the field. These elements can be added in postproduction if needed, but they can't be removed easily.
7. When recording sound effects, record as much as you can as loud as you are able. It may be hard to recreate certain effects.
8. Try to keep each different effect on its own audio channel.
9. Keep everything in stereo in each level of your editing process.
10. If the live, recorded sound doesn't work for whatever reason, don't be afraid to recreate, redub, or remove it.

MASTERING LIGHT

If there is one area that can really help separate your footage from the rest, a craft that represents one of the hardest challenges to any stock video contributor, it is undoubtedly lighting. Being able to light a scene for both technical and stylistic considerations is both an art and a science.

Learning to Light

As we grow older, we all tend to lose the level of awareness we had as a child, but we can still develop a more acute "visual consciousness" at any age. As such, we must try to observe how light illuminates our reality and plays on the physical space around us. What are the characteristics of the artificial light in a kitchen and in a bathroom? What pattern does the sunshine filtering through the curtains make on the living room furniture and the floor? How are people lit in our favorite restaurants? And how are they lit in church? As well, we should examine how other artists see the world, like painters, photographers, and other videographers. It's important to constantly study the visual tradition of our medium and remind ourselves of the business we are in. Effective lighting is one of the best ways to separate you from the others in this field.

> **EFFECTIVE LIGHTING IS ONE OF THE BEST WAYS TO SEPARATE YOU FROM THE OTHERS IN THIS FIELD**

Paintings and photographs are great mediums to study light in as they allow us to linger and analyze. Watching motion pictures demands much quicker observation but has the added benefit of showing you how a moving camera or moving objects in the frame affect how light is perceived.

Finally, we need to learn by doing. Traditionally, documentaries and commercials have been the training ground for many cinematographers. Simultaneously with learning to see light, we must develop a thorough knowledge of lighting tools. We must always instinctively realize what a given light can do for us at a given distance and angle. The more experienced you become with your lighting techniques, the more flexible you can be. When we are learning the tools and training the eyes, we must not lose sight of the reason we are learning all these things: to communicate.

Reading books is also a great way to learn lighting. A couple of my favorites include *The 5 Cs of Cinematography* by Joseph V. Mascelli and *Lighting for Digital Video* by John Jackman.

Another great way to learn is by watching videos. There are tons of great tutorials on YouTube. (There are also a lot of not-so-good tutorials too… so be careful who you learn from.)

In my opinion, however, the absolute BEST way to learn how to light is to go out and watch the pros in action. Eighty percent of everything I know about lighting, I learned by watching a professional director of photography. With this in mind, if you ever have the opportunity to be on set with a professional DP for a day or more, DO IT. You could potentially learn more in a day than you can in a year learning on your own.

Lighting can be an incredibly complex and intricate art form. In an effort to simplify our understanding of lighting for the purposes of shooting stock, I will outline what I consider the four keys to keep in mind as you learn to light for your shoots.

> **THINGS TO REMEMBER:**
> 1. Light intensity
> 2. Color temperature
> 3. Light diffusion (hard vs. soft)
> 4. Light modeling/placement/design

LIGHTING INTENSITY

Let's start with intensity. If the light is really bright, the intensity is high. If it's dim, the intensity is low. It is really quite that simple. Where intensity gets interesting is in determining the proper amount of lighting intensity to not only get a solid exposure for your camera but also do so in a way that looks good to a potential buyer. As a general rule of thumb, it's better to have light with an intensity, or brightness, that is too high rather than too low. You can always get a good exposure by simply closing your aperture on your camera. If you don't have enough light, you'll have to resort to tricks like dialing up the ISO on your camera or even boosting the light artificially with a gain setting in your camera. Either one of these solutions may cause significant grain in your footage and result in clips that are unusable.

STOCK FOOTAGE MILLIONAIRE

Low intensity. © Robb Crocker

Medium intensity. © Robb Crocker

High intensity © Robb Crocker

Choosing Your Equipment

COLOR TEMPERATURE CHART

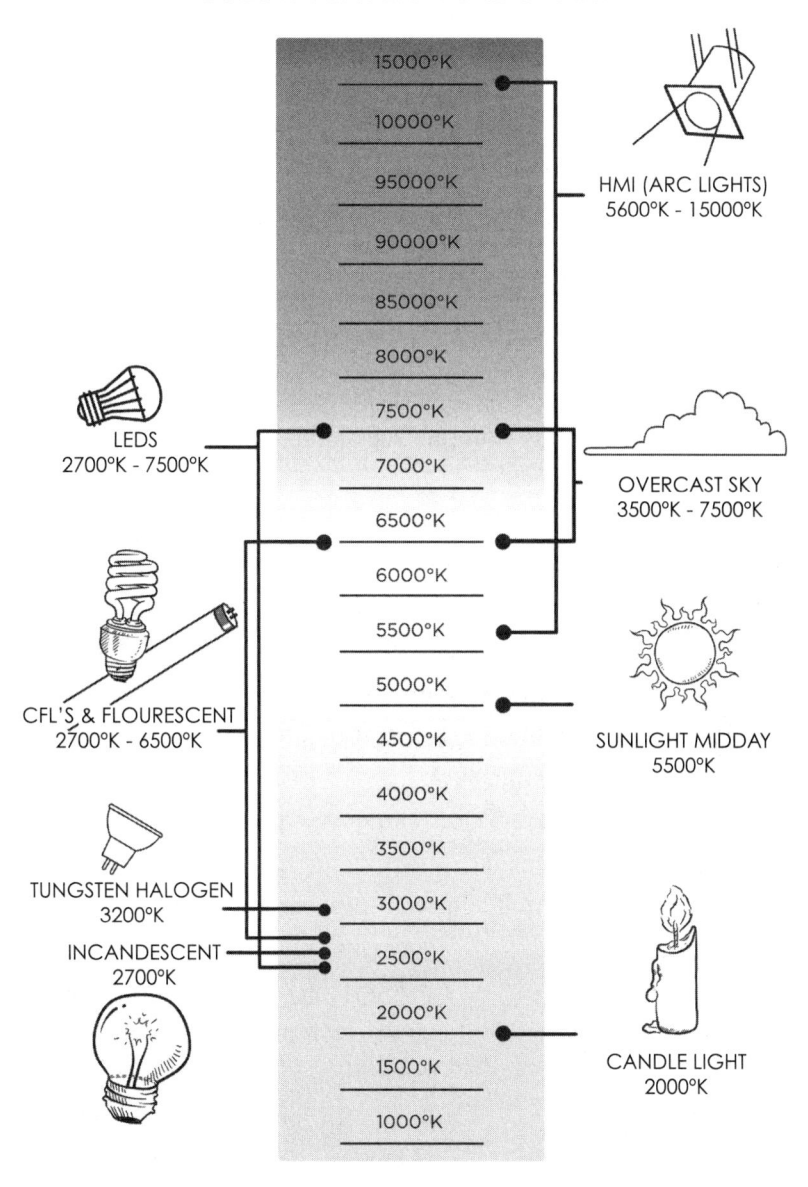

Temperature	Source
15000°K	
10000°K	
95000°K	HMI (ARC LIGHTS) 5600°K - 15000°K
90000°K	
85000°K	
8000°K	
7500°K	
7000°K	OVERCAST SKY 3500°K - 7500°K
6500°K	
6000°K	
5500°K	
5000°K	
4500°K	SUNLIGHT MIDDAY 5500°K
4000°K	
3500°K	
3000°K	
2500°K	
2000°K	
1500°K	CANDLE LIGHT 2000°K
1000°K	

LEDS 2700°K - 7500°K

CFL'S & FLOURESCENT 2700°K - 6500°K

TUNGSTEN HALOGEN 3200°K

INCANDESCENT 2700°K

© Funnelbox

Basic color temperature chart.

61

COLOR TEMPERATURE

Color temperature refers to how blue or orange a light source appears. A simplistic way to describe color temperature is to say that a light is either "cool" or "warm" in color. Color temperature is measured in Kelvin. Natural daylight is considered to be a cool 5600 Kelvin, while standard tungsten lighting instruments are measured at a warm 3200 Kelvin. You can shoot stock footage at any color temperature you want. The important thing to know, however, is what color temperature your lighting sources are and in what color temperature your camera is recording. If you are shooting outside with your camera set to 3200 Kelvin, your footage will look extremely blue. Conversely, if you're shooting inside with artificial light and your camera is set for 5600 Kelvin, your footage will look incredibly orange. Using different color temperatures in the same scene can be done, but it should always be done carefully and with a clear purpose in mind. Like every other part of lighting, it's important to understand how color temperature affects the feeling and mood of a scene so you can use it to your greatest benefit.

LIGHTING DIFFUSION

Light has character, and as such can be hard, soft, or gradations in between. Hard light casts strong shadows and the softest light is shadowless. Hard light is generated from a small source, whereas soft light comes from a large one.

The hardest source of light known in nature is the noonday sun; an overcast sky is the softest. It is as if a diffusion material has been stretched from horizon to horizon. The illumination comes from all directions and cancels out the shadows.

Hard lighting can be made soft through diffusing (like shining a light through a white sheet or frosted gel) and bouncing (like bouncing the light off the ceiling or a piece of white board). Because of the large surface area of the light and the fact that it is so diffused, soft lighting can only become partially directional with the use of flags, grids, or any other opaque material that can block the light from shining in unwanted directions. Creating varying degrees of softness and directionality becomes one of the important methods used to create mood through lighting.

© Robb Crocker

Notice the hard shadow from the model's nose that is cast on her cheek. This hard light source magnifies imperfections on her skin and makes the model feel "hard" or even "mean" to the viewer.

© Robb Crocker

The soft, diffused light in this image is not only flattering to the model, but also makes her seem warm, friendly and approachable to the viewer.

LIGHT MODELING/PLACEMENT/DESIGN

Where you place your lights can have a *massive* effect on the message that is communicated in your footage. An easy example is to think about a kid camping in a tent with a flashlight. When the light is pointed at the roof of the tent and the light has a soft, diffused quality, everything seems safe and comfortable, and the kid's face looks friendly. As soon as that flashlight is held directly under that kid's chin, however, casting long ominous shadows across the cheeks and leaving deep pools of darkness in the eye sockets, that once-friendly face becomes uncomfortably scary. Same light, different placement. It's important to keep this power of placement in mind. You can achieve all kinds of different effects simply by adjusting where you place your lights.

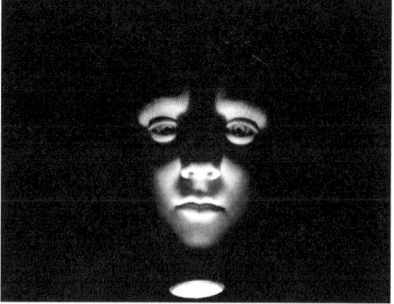

© Robb Crocker

The flashlight bounces off the walls of the tent to diffuse the light on the subject and set a happy tone. The flashlight at a low angle without diffusion sets an ominous tone.

The Three-Point Lighting Foundation

The *Three-Point Lighting Technique* is a standard method used in nearly all visual media including video, film, still photography, and computer-generated imagery. In three-point lighting, a key light is used to illuminate a subject from a high angle near the camera; a slightly lower fill light on the opposite side is used to reduce shadows caused by the

Choosing Your Equipment

key light; and a backlight is used to help separate the subject from the background. It is a simple yet versatile system that forms the basis of most lighting. Variations of three-point lighting in the form of lighting ratios and contrast range allow you to create many different looks. If you don't already, understanding three-point lighting will give you a solid foundation to understanding all lighting.

Naturally you will need three lights to utilize the technique fully, but the principles are still important even if you only use one or two lights. As a rule:

- If you only have one light, it becomes the key.
- If you have two lights, one is the key and the other is either the fill or the backlight.

BASIC THREE POINT LIGHTING DESIGN

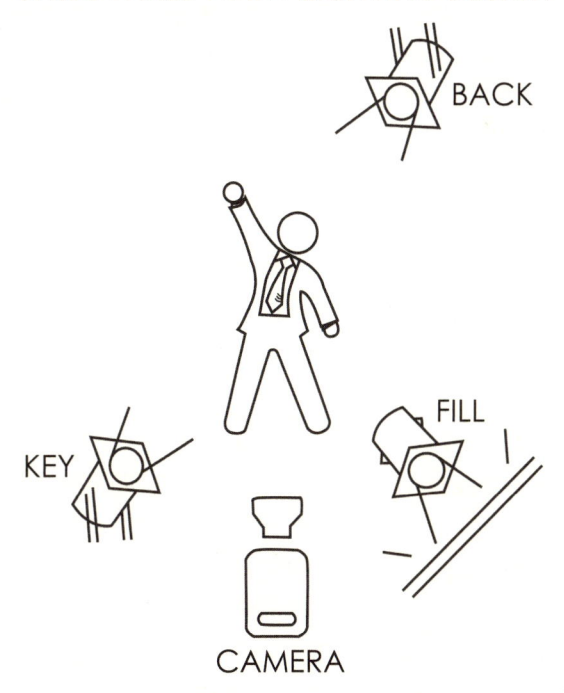

© Funnelbox

A simplified illustration of a standard 3-point lighting set up.

KEY LIGHT

This is the main light. It is usually the strongest and has the most influence on the look of the scene. It is placed to one side of the camera/subject so this side is well lit and the other side has some shadow. The quality of the key light can be either hard or soft, depending on the look you want and the feeling or mood you want to convey.

© Robb Crocker

Keylight with the added fill light

FILL LIGHT

This is the secondary light and is placed on the opposite side of the key light. It is used to fill the shadows created by the key. The quality of the fill light can also be hard or soft, but in most situations, it tends to be on the softer side and a little less bright than the key. To achieve this, you can move the light farther away from your subject, reflect the light off of a reflective surface, or use a diffusion material in front of the light.

The fill light is a very important light. It not only helps to ensure that you get a good exposure, but it also plays a critical role in helping to set the mood in your shot. For instance, if your fill light is extremely dim, the shadows on your subject will be dark and the shot

Choosing Your Equipment

Diffused keylight only.

Fill light only.

Back light only.

67

will have a lot of contrast, conveying a sense of moodiness or drama. If your fill light is nearly as bright as the key light, however, there will be almost no shadows, and the evenly lit scene will feel much more bright and friendly.

BACKLIGHT, AKA "RIM LIGHT"

The backlight is placed behind the subject to light it from the rear. Rather than providing direct lighting (like the key and fill), its purpose is to provide definition and subtle highlights around the subject's outlines. This helps separate the subject from the background and provide a three-dimensional look.

© Robb Crocker

Keylight, fill light, and the added backlight.

Traditionally, a backlight fulfills the function of separating people from the background. Depending on the angle, these accentuating, textural lights have many names. **Backlight** usually means a light directly behind the subject in line with the lens. A backlight that does not indicate the source but just lights the hair is appropriately called the *hair light*. Also from the back comes the *rim light*, which simply adds a thin rim of light to the subject. The next light farther to the side is the **kicker**, which gives a certain sheen to the cheek as seen from the camera position. While there are specific differences in the positioning in these lights, in practice the terms for these lighting positions are used less precisely and sometimes interchangeably. The backlight to one person may mean the rim light or the kicker to another. Every motion picture lighting professional seems to have their own set of terms and understanding of what those mean.

This variety of light directions represents part of the palette of the cinematographer, to be used judiciously when and where it is needed. Incidentally, backlighting need not be a hard, directional light. I often use soft, diffused light to create the effects of separation and light rim on a subject.

Beyond the Three-Point Setup

In addition to the standard three-point lighting setup, there are many other types of lights that pros use to help light their footage. We'll go over a few of them here.

EYE LIGHT

The eyes, it is often said, are the windows of the soul, and great care should be taken to show the eyes of the main actors in your stock footage. Some lighting styles, like the overall soft light from an overcast sky, will often require an eye light to help bring out the life in your talent's eyes. To obtain a clear sparkle in the eye, such light will usually be situated very close to the lens. But due to the curvature of the eye, some people's eyes will pick up an eye light from the side as well.

WASH

A wash light simply washes a splash of light on a background or background object.

© Uberstock

The added light in the background helps to illuminate the old pipes and chain link fence to give the image a more "gritty" feel.

LIGHT SOURCES

Deciding on light sources involves the aesthetic philosophy of the cinematographer. In traditional cinematography circles, there are two basic philosophies towards lighting. The naturalistic school of lighting is called Naturalism and follows the natural, logically established sources of light in the scene. For instance, if you are shooting a shot outdoors and there is a hard, direct sunlight shining from behind your subject, you let the face naturally remain in relative shadow. Pictorialism, on the other hand, uses light angles that focus on creating the most pleasing image to the eye regardless of the natural law of the surroundings. So, in the previous example, a cinematographer might shine an equally bright light from the front of a subject to get a bright, even exposure of the face, in spite of the fact that the sun is clearly shining from behind.

Choosing Your Equipment

© Robb Crocker

A diffused back light and a bright gold fill light make a pleasing, but very unnatural image. This is a good example of "Pictoralism."

© Robb Crocker

This image is representative of "Naturalism." There is nothing other than the hard sun shining on the model from behind. The ambient light is not strong enough to eliminate the shadow opposite the sun.

© Robb Crocker

This is my favorite compromise in natural lighting. The sun serves as a warm and powerful back light, and the shadows are filled by reflecting some of that same light onto the model with a diffused bounce board.

But there doesn't have to be cut-and-dry division between these two approaches. It is more a matter of give and take, considering the most logical source of natural light, but also the compositional requirements of lighting the frame.

Generally, most cinematographers believe in justifying the source of light. I believe, too, that the current aesthetic buyers are looking for is one that leads towards authenticity and realism, which means that a more naturalistic lighting style tends to sell better. Like most trends do, however, the trend towards naturalism is likely to change at some point.

LIGHTING INSTRUMENTS

Over the years, professional lighting designers, cinematographers, and professional gaffers have designed a vast array of lighting instruments to produce both hard and soft lights. It may be helpful here to discuss the different types of fixtures and the basic categories that these instruments fall into: **open-faced, lensed, fluorescents, HMI, Softlights**, and other **specialty instruments**. I'm also going to give you some ideas on how to go about finding some DIY alternatives.

Professional LED Light Panels

Many people would argue that LED lights are the future of video lighting kits. For the little amount of energy they consume, LEDs are relatively bright and they last longer than other portable lights when running on battery power. Because they draw less power, they also produce less heat and are more durable than other bulbs overall. These features combined with the tendency for LED fixtures to be lightweight, make them ideal in terms of portability. We own a number of LED panels and love their portability, durability, and low-power draw.

Choosing Your Equipment

When choosing an LED light, you should consider two important features: color temperature and brightness. The standard color temperature for indoor light is 3200K, or tungsten-balanced. Outdoor light is 5600K, or daylight-balanced. LED lights come in a range of temperatures, so depending on what you're shooting, you'll need to buy an LED light accordingly or purchase filters. Some of the more versatile models have adjustable color temperatures, which eliminates the need for gels or filters all together. You might also keep an eye out for the CRI rating on the light. This is a scale from one to one hundred that quantifies how true-to-life the colors illuminated by this light source will be. The higher the number, the truer the color.

© Shutterstock | Oleksandr Kostiuchenko

LED Light Panel

Generally speaking, LED lights are *not* as bright as their incandescent or halogen counterparts. But, if you invest the capital, you can find high-quality LED panels that shine at 3000-7500 lumens or brighter, which is equivalent to a 200-500-watt tungsten bulb. One drawback of the LED panels though, is that the light source is very directional and can be somewhat harsh.

Currently, it could be said that the biggest downside of going with an LED solution is the cost. However, the numbers of affordable LED options are growing as I write. Research different models carefully and be aware of the following cons when considering less-expensive models: low CRI rates, color shifting over time, insufficient lumens per square meter (lux), and flicker.

Professional Open-Faced Lights

Open-faced tungsten lighting instruments are often regarded as the most basic instrument with a bulb and some sort of reflector. These lights can vary from a simple, inexpensive photoflood reflector that you might find on eBay, all the way up to a durable, professional open-face such as an Arri or Mole. These are great entry-level units, and a simple set of three could easily get you started with shooting stock footage. Focusing is allowed through the simple mechanism of moving the bulb backward and forward in the reflector. When positioned near the front, the light throws a wide beam; when positioned near the rear, it becomes a tighter, more focused beam. Because of the simple construction, many open-faced units can also cast a slight double edge to shadows, so if you have a choice, they may be better suited for sets and backgrounds as opposed to facial closeups. We have a number of open-faced units and use them primarily for general fill lights and wash lights for backgrounds and for bringing up the general lighting ambience in a scene.

© Shutterstock ı ConstantinosZ

Open-faced tungsten light.

Professional Lensed Instruments

These are most commonly tungsten lighting instruments. But more and more, we're seeing large LED bulbs replacing the hot incandescent globes that have been used since the early 1900s. These lensed instruments simply have a beam that is focused by a glass lens rather than a reflector. Usually a reflector of some sort is used as well, but it plays a lesser role in the composition of the instrument. Fresnels are the nearly ubiquitous and affordable lensed light that you will most often encounter. Fresnels are available from many, many providers and range from the very, very small (100W) all the way up to the 24-inch Mole Solarspot (10,000W). As cameras become more and more sensitive, the light levels have decreased and with them, the needed power. It is entirely possible for a great stock shooter to use only 500W, 650W and 1,000W units and make a very, very good living in stock footage.

A lensed Fresnel light.

© Shutterstock ı Hurst Photo

Naturally, Fresnels aren't the only type of lensed instrument available. The Leko, named for the shape of the reflector, projects a sharp beam, almost like a spotlight, with a very even light distribution. Cutouts can be inserted into the body to project different patterns. Additionally, the Dedolight is popular (although it can be a bit pricey) because of its small size, which dramatically helps portability as well as the nice, even light throw.

We have a full arsenal of Fresnel lights ranging from 150W to 2,000W. We also have a couple of Leko lights for special lighting situations and a Dedolight kit with three small, but very powerful lights that we use when in tight quarters.

Professional Fluorescents

Fluorescents are the definition of the soft diffused light that radiates in all directions. They have a relatively short, effective throw and are best used close to the subject. Another selling point is their dramatically lower energy consumption and their cooler operating temperatures. Incandescent lighting can get very, VERY hot and can burn up energy costs (and cooling costs to offset the heat!) very quickly.

A great-selling, versatile and strong fluorescent instrument is the Diva-Lite made by Kino Flo. These are simply a bank of color-balanced tubes operated by a dimmable ballast. We have several of these on hand and use them regularly in our stock footage shoots.

Professional HMI (Arc Lights)

HMIs are extremely powerful daylight-balanced lighting instruments. They are useful when trying to supplement the natural light of the sun, or when lighting for high-speed shooting. The one disadvantage to HMI lighting instruments remains the fact that they must run off a special power supply known as a ballast. Similar to what a welder would use, the role of a ballast is to limit the amperage that runs through the arc of the bulb. Though these ballasts have gotten smaller, cheaper, and easier to move, they still provide an additional piece of equipment and cost for the stock video shooter. And if the ballast isn't new enough, or calibrated correctly, it can cause the light to flicker in your shots if you are shooting at various different frame rates. HMIs are expensive, but very useful for shooting due to their power and natural daylight color balance. We use five different HMIs on a fairly regular basis.

DIY Alternatives

With a little imagination and ingenuity, you can find all kinds of DIY solutions for lighting your scenes. I've purchased a ton of compact florescent lightbulbs (CFLs) in all kinds of different color temperatures to use in any number of shoots. I've built light boxes with CFLs and rigid insulation. I've built soft spots with giant CFLs, aluminum duct pipe and aluminum tape. I've even used high-powered LED flashlights reflected off of a white piece of cardboard. Do a search of DIY video lights on Google, and you'll find an abundant supply of ideas.

ADDITIONAL LIGHTING TIPS:

- Ensure you are always aware of light. Like a great photographer, a top-notch stock videographer is at all times aware of the light. What way is the sun about to set? How will the passing clouds impact the lighting on your models? As you move between rooms of a house—or from outdoors to indoors—what needs to be accounted for?
- When shooting outside in natural light, respect the old truism: The only light worth shooting by is from dawn until ten o'clock in the morning or four o'clock in the afternoon until sunset. That's an old adage that is well worth keeping fresh in your mind. In most cas-

es, whenever possible, avoid the harsh overhead light of noon.

- To produce a softer light with diffusion, you can shine your light through any number of materials, from plastic sheets, silk, and bleached muslin, to a vast choice of sophisticated diffusers offered by companies such as Rosco and Lee.
- Reflecting or bouncing light is another great way to produce a soft source. Simply use a large reflective surface to redirect light toward your subject. When the reflecting surface is large and matte in texture, it will provide an extremely soft light. Keep in mind, however, that its throw will be rather limited. Any white wall or ceiling can be utilized for bouncing light, but there is also a range of materials used specifically for this purpose in the field of cinematography. Styrofoam bead boards are considered to have the most matte surface and therefore reflect the softest light. They are extremely lightweight and can be easily broken into different shapes, but they cannot be bent. Next in softness are show cards, also known as art cards. They have a very good white on one side and black on the other. Slightly less white and with a bit more sheen are foamcore boards, which come in larger sizes (4'x8') than show cards. They can be bent into a corner. They are very good when a little more direction for the light is needed. You can find most of these materials at either a building materials store or art supply store.

SIX

Finding, Casting, and Directing Talent

IF YOU'RE GOING TO SPEND time, money, and resources producing stock footage, you need to make sure it will be footage worth buying. If you are planning on shooting footage that involves people, a huge part of determining whether it will be worth buying is predicated on how good the talent is. Let me repeat that: If you want to produce footage that sells, you *must* employ great talent.

Most buyers of stock footage are looking for an idealized image of people for the videos they are producing. That means healthy, happy, friendly, good-looking people. It isn't reality, as there are many more average-looking, unhealthy people in society (especially in the United States) than there are the types of people used in advertisements. But the fact of the matter is, this idealized image of society is what sells. There are, of course, exceptions to this rule, like when a buyer is looking specifically for a shot of someone who is overweight, "ugly," "goofy," or maybe "mean-looking." By and large, however, we see the greatest demand for footage with talent that looks healthy, happy, friendly and above-all, good-looking.

How people look, though, is only part of the equation when it comes to footage. They also have to be able to act naturally in front of the camera. Stock-footage models and talent don't pose like they might for still photos. And viewers can tell in an instant when the talent isn't acting naturally in stock footage. If the footage looks staged, stiff, or over the top, it won't garner big sales numbers. That's why it's so important to find talent that is both comfortable in front of a camera and able to deliver an authentic, natural-looking performance.

> IF YOU WANT TO PRODUCE FOOTAGE THAT SELLS, YOU *MUST* EMPLOY GREAT TALENT.

Remember, all things being equal, attractive talent will always outsell average-looking talent. It's not politically correct. It may not even be fair. But unfortunately, it's the truth.

FINDING TALENT

First off, let's talk about your resources for finding great (ideally inexpensive or free) talent.

Friends and Family

As hesitant as I am to recommend this, especially right after expressing how important high-quality talent is in your stock-footage production efforts, the quickest and easiest source of talent is probably your family and friends. Now, if you are lucky enough to have happy, healthy, friendly, good-looking people as friends, who are comfortable in front of a camera and can act naturally while a camera is in their face, you've hit the stock-footage producer's jackpot. (Seriously, it's like winning the lottery.) Sign them up and start shooting. For the rest of us, we'll need to pick and choose which of our family and friends might make good subjects for our stock-footage productions. There are obviously plusses and minuses to this strategy. On the positive side, you'll probably be able to hire friends and family for a pretty good rate, maybe even free. You'll also get an opportunity to practice your craft in a low-pressure environment with people who you are both comfortable around and who won't be inclined to judge you or your skills. This is especially nice if you're just getting started. Some of my best-selling footage is of my daughter, my daughter and wife together, and three of our friends' daughters walking in a field. I probably spent a total of $150 on talent for this footage that has generated well over $30,000 in earnings for me.

> UTILIZING FRIENDS AND FAMILY FOR TALENT *CAN* BE A GREAT WAY TO GO WHEN SHOOTING STOCK FOOTAGE.

The downside of using friends and family is that they more than likely aren't model-worthy, or able to give you those authentic, believable performances on cue. (In my opinion, this isn't as big an issue with small children, as they are almost all model-worthy and can be coached to act naturally by simply letting them act naturally. I'll touch more on this later.) Also, because they probably aren't being paid, friends and family might not feel much of an obligation to work with you as long as you may need them to. If they get tired, bored, or just plain restless, there's a good chance you might lose them before you get the shots you need. (There have been plenty of times when one of my toddler-aged offspring has cut short what was supposed to be a spectacular shoot during the magic hour.)

When all is said and done, however, utilizing friends and family for talent *can* be a great way to go when shooting stock footage.

The Internet

Websites like Craigslist.com and ModelMayhem.com can be a great resource for finding talent. As with everything in life, these have their pluses and minuses. The positives of using websites like these include the ability to reach a large number of people at any time of day, relatively quickly and easily. There is also some really good talent that regularly scan websites like these for gigs like the one you're casting for. The price can also be very right as well. Because you're negotiating directly with the talent, you're often able to get a very reasonable rate for their services and don't have to pay any agency fees or markups. Sometimes, you can find talent who are just getting started and willing to trade their acting services for some of the finished footage to use in their demo reels. I've hired a ton of great talent through both Craigslist.com and ModelMayhem.com and continue to utilize those channels on a regular basis.

> MEET THE TALENT IN-PERSON BEFORE COMMITTING TO HIRING THEM FOR A SHOOT

There is a downside to this approach, however. One thing to consider is that, because these aren't professional channels to acquire talent, sometimes you can run into people who are less than professional. Specifically, they may show up late, they may come unprepared or without proper wardrobe, or they may not even show up at all. Another thing to keep in mind is that they may have very little acting or on-camera experience. If this is the case and you've never worked with them before, you might end up getting a real dud but still have to pay for the time they committed to working for you. It's important to keep this in mind when casting via the Internet. Whenever possible, I like to meet the talent in-person before committing to hiring them for a shoot. It gives me an opportunity to meet them, verify that they actually look as good in person as they do in their headshot, and get a feel for their ability. If you make this a standard practice, you should have pretty good luck casting through these channels.

Talent Agencies and Casting Directors

Once you are ready to spend less time looking for talent yourself and are willing to pay others to do that for you, you can engage a talent agency or casting director. A talent agent represents a roster of professional models and/or actors. They work on the talent's behalf to find them work. In exchange, they charge the person hiring the talent (you) a small fee and take a percentage of the fee earned by the talent.

If you live in, or near, a larger metropolitan area (I happen to be in Portland, Oregon—large, but by no means massive) you can find a list of talent agencies in a quick Internet search. Locally, you can often find them listed under Talent Agencies, Modeling Agencies and the like. A quick Google search should pull up a variety of agencies that can help you. Compare prices, shop around, and find one that makes you feel comfortable in what you are trying to achieve. It might behoove you to find one with young talent or new talent with less experience who are willing to work for a bit less than the talent at larger, more established agencies. This is especially true if you are just getting started.

A casting director is an individual who works with multiple talent agencies to find talent on your behalf. They are not constrained by a single agency's roster of talent but are able to go to multiple sources to get just the right talent for what you need. Casting directors are people whose livelihood depends on keeping up-to-date information on the actors and models available in your particular geography. A casting director has no special loyalty to any specific actor/actress or talent agencies and can call on anyone, from anywhere to audition for a part.

They can also help you determine a fair rate to pay for the talent you want and can help in negotiating rates for that talent. This can be very beneficial, as many first-time stock shooters may not have an idea what they should expect to pay for talent. The casting director is usually compensated on a daily or an hourly rate. Sometimes, however, you can negotiate with them to do the work for a flat fee. If you can find a casting director who understands what you are trying to achieve and is willing to work with your budget, it makes a lot of sense to use one. If, on the other hand, you aren't able to find one who you think you can work with, you can do that work yourself by calling and working with multiple agencies.

> FIRST-TIME STOCK SHOOTERS MAY NOT HAVE AN IDEA WHAT THEY SHOULD EXPECT TO PAY FOR TALENT

MODEL RELEASES

A common question that producers have about shooting stock footage is: When do I need to get a model release form signed? The answer to that question has actually changed over the years. It used to be that you only needed a release form if the model was easily identifiable. Now, if the model is identifiable *in any way*, even by context, a release is required. For example, silhouettes, tattoos, specific settings, or locations all give context that might make the subject recognizable to viewers. When children are involved, or other sensitive subject matter like partial nudity, release requirements are even more stringent. If the model is NOT the subject of the shot, *and* they do NOT have *any* defining features, then a release may not be required. However, a good rule of thumb is, whether friend, family, or pro, just have them sign a release form. No matter which stock agency you choose, if your subject is identifiable in any way, they are all going to require a model release form to be submitted along with your clip.

Most stock agencies provide release forms that can be downloaded from their websites. If you're going to create your own form, here's a general example for your consideration. (I am not an attorney, and

Finding, Casting, and Directing Talent

don't represent this example to be a legally binding document for you to use. Before using ANY release form, make sure to get it checked out by your own legal council.)

MODEL RELEASE

For good and valuable Consideration herein acknowledged as received, and by signing this release I hereby give the Photographer/Filmmaker and Assigns my permission to license the Images and to use the Images in any Media for any purpose (except pornographic or defamatory) which may include, among others, advertising, promotion, marketing and packaging for any product or service. I agree that the Images may be combined with other images, text and graphics, and cropped, altered or modified. I acknowledge as indicated below, but understand that other ethnicities may be associated with Images of me by the Photographer/Filmmaker and/or Assigns for descriptive purposes.

I agree that I have no rights to the Images, and all rights to the Images belong to the Photographer/Filmmaker and Assigns. I acknowledge and agree that I have no further right to additional Consideration or accounting, and that I will make no further claim for any reason to Photographer/Filmmaker and/or Assigns. I agree that this release is irrevocable, worldwide and perpetual, and will be governed by the laws of the **State of Oregon**.

I represent and warrant that I am at least 18 years of age and have the full legal capacity to execute this release.

Definitions:
"MODEL" means me and includes my appearance, likeness and form.
"MEDIA" means all media including digital, electronic, print, television, film and other media now known or to be invented.
"PHOTOGRAPHER/FILMMAKER" means photographer, illustrator, filmmaker or cinematographer, or any other person or entity photographing or recording me.
"ASSIGNS" means a person or any company to whom Photographer/Filmmaker has assigned or licensed rights under this release as well as the licensees of any such person or company.
"IMAGES" means all photographs, film or recording taken of me as part of the Shoot.
"CONSIDERATION" means something of value I have received in exchange for the rights granted by me in this release.
"SHOOT" means the photographic or film session described in this form.
"PARENT" means the parent and/or legal guardian of the Model. Parent and Model are referred to together as "we" and "us" in this release.

Name (print): _____
Address: _____
City: _____ State: _____
Country: _____ Zip: _____
Phone: _____ Email: _____
Date of Birth: _____
Signature: _____ Date: _____

Parent(s) or Guardian(s) (if a person is a minor or lacks capacity in the jurisdiction of residence.) Parent warrants and represents that Parent is the legal guardian of Model, and has the full legal capacity to consent to the Shoot and to execute this release OF ALL RIGHTS IN MODEL'S IMAGES.

Name (print): _____
Address: _____
City: _____ State: _____
Country: _____ Zip: _____
Phone: _____ Email: _____
Signature: _____ Date: _____

Invoice (if applicable)
Rate: _____ per Hour/Day (circle one)
Number of Hours/Days: _____
Invoice Total: _____

Additional Terms:
_____
_____
_____
_____
_____

Attach Visual Reference of Model here: (Optional)

Photographer/Filmmaker Information
Name (print): _____
Address: _____
City: _____ State: _____
Country: _____ Zip: _____
Phone: _____ Email: _____
Shoot Date: _____
Shoot Description: _____
Signature: _____ Date: _____

Witness (Note: All persons signing and witnessing must be of legal age and capacity in the area in which this Release is signed. A person cannot witness their own release.)

Name (print): _____
Signature: _____

© Funnelbox

Example of a fairly standard model release.

DIRECTING YOUR TALENT

We talked about the importance of finding and casting great talent, and securing this talent is obviously very important. That said, where you really make money as a stock-footage producer lies in how you work with and direct that talent. Directing talent is more of an art than science. Getting good at directing takes practice. Lots of practice. That said, there are certainly tips, tricks, and techniques that can be quickly learned to help shorten your learning curve when it comes to successfully directing your talent.

Let's start with a few general rules when it comes to working with talent. First, keep your shoots as light and fun as possible. One of the best aspects of producing stock footage is that you don't have a paying client breathing down your neck. With the burden of someone else's expectations off of your back, you can afford to take some extra time to help your talent feel as relaxed and comfortable as possible. Keep it light. Don't get too serious. If your talent messes up a direction or action, let them know that it's no big deal, and have them do it again. Try to make sure that they are having fun. If you can pull this off, your footage will look much more authentic and will result in increased sales.

> **GETTING GOOD AT DIRECTING TAKES PRACTICE.**

ROBB'S RULES

RULES FOR DIRECTING TALENT:

1. Keep it light, keep it fun.
2. Don't expect people to pretend or act, instead, encourage them to simply act naturally.
3. Direct loosely and wait for genuine emotion to result.

As much as possible, I try hard not to ask my talent to act. It may seem counter-intuitive, but I don't really want people to act. I want them to act naturally. So, what does this mean? It means that, rather than asking the talent to think about a feeling or emotion, I have them perform a very specific action or course of action. For instance, if I want to capture some genuine moments of shared joy between a dad and young daughter, I might ask them to hold hands, skip twenty feet towards the camera, then stop and have the dad pick up the daughter and swing her around in his arms two times before letting her down where she can give him a kiss on the cheek. What inevitably happens is that they screw it up. But that's okay. Because I know that when they do, I'll probably get a very genuine bit of laughter and smiles. That's what I'm really after anyway. I don't care all that much if they get the skipping right or the kiss on the cheek perfect. If they do, that's a bonus. But again, what I'm really looking to do is capture the emotion. This is what stock footage buyers are looking for.

I've learned to give talent specific instruction to help connote all kinds of feelings and emotions in my stock footage, everything from the power pose of an executive, to the sorrow of a grieving woman. You can elicit these types of emotions as well as using this type of loose directing style. All it takes is a bit of forethought and some practice.

The Day of Shooting

On the day of shooting, there are a few things I do to help ensure a successful shoot. When the talent arrives, the first thing I do is greet them warmly and ask them to sign a talent release form. Then I talk with them about the expectations for the shoot. We discuss how long the shoot is scheduled to last, for how long and how often I'll need them, and with whom else they may be acting and interacting with on camera. After that, if we're using a wardrobe provided by the talent, I'll review and select their wardrobe from the options they brought with them. Once they get changed and in wardrobe, I'll bring all of the talent together to talk about what we are looking to accomplish for the shoot. We'll talk about the kinds of things we will have them do and the kinds of feelings and emotions we want to convey through the footage. I'll also introduce them to any of the crew working on set. Again, I want to make the talent as relaxed and comfortable as possible, and knowing the people with whom you are working helps.

> **THINGS TO REMEMBER:**
> **SHOOT DAY**
>
> - Get releases signed
> - Go over expectations for the shoot with talent
> - Review talent wardrobe
> - Make introductions to the crew and talent
> - Situate talent, help them relax
> - Rehearse the action
> - Start rolling once they're relaxed
> - Always give positive feedback and gentle direction after each take

Once you've got your lights and camera ready to roll, get your talent situated in the location you want. Again, try to be as friendly and accommodating as possible. Once in their spot, ask them to "shake it out." Have them shake out their arms and legs and loosen up their neck, to help them relieve any pent up tension. And finally, before starting the shoot, have them take one huge deep breath *with* you. By doing this together, at the same time, this helps to relieve tension in both you and your talent and acts as a visual and psychological connector between the two of you as friends and allies.

Sometimes, but not always, I'll rehearse whatever action I want them to perform a couple of times before I roll the camera. It really depends on the complexity of the shot. The red light on the camera, the quietness of the set, and the talent being on for the first time can make them uncomfortable, so sometimes a rehearsal or two can help. Once I get a realistic performance out of them, I'll often roll the camera without telling them. In doing so, I don't make a big deal out of the fact that we've started, which can sometimes add unnecessary pressure on the talent.

Once they complete the action I've given them, I simply acknowledge them with a positive response and give them some additional direction on how I'd like it to be done again but differently. I repeat this process until I get what I feel is a good take. I then make adjustments either to the camera or action and repeat the process again.

Body Language and Gestures

Body language is of utmost importance in any successful stock video. The physical relationship and the movements of people in your footage should send a clear and direct message to your viewers. Specifically, I want to talk about two elements when it comes to body language: the use of authentic gestures and the physical spacing of talent in your scenes.

When considering the authenticity or appropriateness of the body language to the role of the person in the video clip, you should ask yourself: Is the person or relationship believable? If you have to think about it, the video won't work. Again, here is a vital difference between video and photo: You will need to coax out of your talent ten to thirty seconds of believable, authentic action and emotion. You aren't able to simply hope for a split second of magic; you'll need to sustain it

> BODY LANGUAGE IS OF UTMOST IMPORTANCE IN ANY SUCCESSFUL STOCK VIDEO.

as a team, both videographer AND actor/actresses for over ten seconds. This is one of the reasons I like to give talent specific actions to execute, rather than asking them to pretend (aka act) like they are doing something.

It's also important to consider the physical space that is being conveyed in the clip; specifically, is it believable? If you are shooting a family scene, do they appear to have appropriately close enough spacing? Also, spatial relationships imply hierarchy and role. Are you able to quickly understand from pure physical positioning alone who is in charge in the group or scene that you are shooting? Likewise, are you able to see the subordinates and how they are sitting around a boardroom or conference room table? Is it readily apparent what message you are looking to convey? And always remember, often what looks right on-camera feels very awkward and contrived in real life.

> **OFTEN WHAT LOOKS RIGHT ON-CAMERA FEELS VERY AWKWARD AND CONTRIVED IN REAL LIFE**

DIRECTING: USING FOREGROUND AND BACKGROUND

While the action of the video clip normally takes place in the foreground, close to the camera, the director must not neglect the background. Select an interesting setting for the shot, and, if appropriate, populate the scene with people who are doing something appropriate in the background to help breathe life and authenticity into the footage.

Another way to breathe life and believability into your footage is to use foreground action *between* the camera and your subject matter. If you want that slice-of-life feel, ensure that, when appropriate, people and things occasionally wander between your camera and your subject matter. Done thoughtfully and with proper composition and timing, this foreground action adds life and realism to your footage and helps to prevent it from feeling stale and staged.

DIRECTING CHILDREN

When looking for the perfect child for your next shoot, make sure you audition him or her before you cast the child in the part. If your neighbor, wife, or girlfriend insists you use "their little blossom," make sure he or she can act. Good-looking kids are easy to find; talented ones are more difficult.

It sometimes helps to have the child involved in as many aspects of the production as necessary. Tell him or her the purpose of what you're doing, describe the various roles of the crew, and introduce the child to everyone. Again, it helps to make the child feel more comfortable around the lights, camera, and crew if they feel everyone on set is their friend.

Some kids have acted before, and many have not. You will quickly find out if they have if you audition them. (Which you should, whenever possible.) Regardless, you should treat all children the same—professional or amateur. It's exciting to be in front of the camera. Do your best to make it a fun experience for them. Let the kids wear makeup before being shot as it makes them feel more grown up. And again, it sometimes makes sense to rehearse the action several times before the cameras roll. This can help to put them at ease before you actually begin. During this dry run, do everything exactly like the actual shoot so they know what to expect.

> **BREATHE LIFE AND BELIEVABILITY INTO YOUR FOOTAGE**

> **THINGS TO REMEMBER:**
> **WHEN DIRECTING CHILDREN**
>
> - Audition ahead of time
> - Make everyone on set their friend
> - Show them the camera and lights, get them comfortable on set
> - Treat all the same, pro or amateur
> - Make the experience as fun as possible
> - Make sure they know exactly what to expect
> - Maintain authority; you are in control
> - They make a mistake? No big deal!
> - Involve parents when coaching the unruly
> - Keep the shoot short
> - Keep the child well fed
> - Appreciate what they do right

It's also important to make sure each child knows that you are in control. Don't talk down to them, but make sure they know exactly what is expected from them. If you relinquish authority early on in an effort to appease them, you may never get it back again.

It's also important to emphasize that if a child makes a mistake, don't make a big deal out of it. Keep rehearsing, if necessary, until you get the performance you are after. If that still doesn't happen, don't embarrass him or her in front of everyone. Ask the kid if he or she would like a break and discuss the problem privately. If the child is impossible, discretely ask the parents to talk to the child. Kids are kids, but they have moods just like adults. Make sure you are with the parents when they explain what the child should do. Don't work them too long, as they can tend to get cranky and uncooperative. And make sure to feed them often (but stay away from sugary snacks), and complement them when they do something correctly. There is an old adage that states, "What you appreciate, appreciates." If you appreciate them for doing things right, you'll tend to get more of that behavior. If, on the other hand, you only recognize everything they are doing wrong, well…

WORKING WITH PEOPLE WHO ARE NOT ACTORS

Over the last seven years of shooting stock footage, as well as from my 17-plus years of experience shooting client projects of all sorts, I've compiled a list of mistakes directors often make in working with people who are not actors.

- **Treating amateurs like pros.** Most amateur talent can do a reasonably good job in front of a camera if you give them some very specific physical actions to accomplish. As soon as you start asking them to think about and communicate emotion through their acting, things will fall apart quickly. Set up a situation where your amateur talent can behave naturally, and you'll get much better results.
- **Failure to explain what you're doing and how long it will take.** Even when you are working with paid actors, common courtesy demands a realistic explanation of the task and the time it will take.
- **Failure to discuss wardrobe and makeup.** As a general rule of thumb, make sure EVERYONE is on the same page when it comes to wardrobe. Make sure everyone knows what the talent is expected to bring to the shoot and wear. This will help to alleviate any unfortunate clothing mishaps. Just be sure to talk about it and ask everyone to bring *at least* three changes of

clothes. (I usually ask them to bring at least five options.)

- **Putting unnecessary pressure on the talent.** I don't ever like to lie, but sometimes, when it comes to preserving a talent's confidence and focus, I might be inclined to tell a white lie by blaming the need for a retake on a technical glitch. If your talent is having repeated issues with getting an action or instruction correct due to nerves, it sometimes makes sense to blame something other than their acting ability. The self-confidence of many first-time actors and actresses can feel nervous when they are asked to retake a scene over and over if they feel they are the reason for the repetition.

- **Stopping the process to get them to do it right.** Anything that calls repeated and unnecessary attention to people who are not actors is another way of putting pressure on them for a performance. I've found that calling attention to errors just tends to magnify them and almost always has the adverse effect of what I'm trying to accomplish.

- **Letting the crew command.** When the crew starts to give directions to the people you are shooting, things can quickly get out of hand. If you are fortunate enough to have some help on the scene, whether holding lights or steadying your camera, or bouncing fill light, make sure they understand that you are in control on the set and that no comments should be made directly to the talent without first consulting you. Comments from the peanut gallery can only add confusion, tension, and pressure on amateur talent. Make sure the only director on set is you.

WORKING WITH ANIMALS AND TODDLERS

There are always special considerations that you need to keep in mind when working with the "untrainables," namely untrained animals and toddlers. Toddlers and untrained animals are simply not capable of responding to direction much beyond the one-word commands that I tend to employ.

First, if you are using both children and animals in the same scene, check to see if your head is screwed on straight. (Really, are you crazy?) If it is, then you'll also need to check to see if there are allergies to consider. Are your children comfortable with cats, dogs, or other animals? Do they have pets at home, or is this the first four-legged creature they have ever seen? If your children are afraid of the animals, quickly determine how you will adjust to your new reality.

> DO EVERYTHING IN YOUR POWER TO KEEP THINGS MOVING

Second, if you want lively animals during your scene, don't feed them immediately before a shoot. Not unlike people, once the food hits the stomach, their energy level drops and they won't be as alert as you would have liked. Bits of food also can serve as bait and rewards once they accomplish what you are asking them to do. If you DO want a drowsy animal (perhaps by the fireside or by each other in a cuddly pose), if possible, make the food a bit warm and it will sometimes calm the animal and induce an appropriate amount of drowsiness.

If you're shooting toddlers, keep them well fed and make sure they always have something to either play with or look at. They don't react well to hunger, or boredom. It helps to have an assistant who can distract them long enough for you to get that perfect shot.

Finally, you should do everything in your power to keep things moving. Be as quick as you professionally can be. You might capture some fantastic, spontaneous footage, but I'll warn you, getting sustained shots longer than 10 seconds in length can be very difficult. I have repeatedly filmed my daughters (one when she was only several hours old) and have had great success selling clips of them from newborns all the way through age eight. But, for the most part, those clips are less than 15 seconds in length. It's just very, very difficult to get more than 10 seconds of quality, sustained action from young children. So, whatever you do, make sure you're ready to shoot and move quickly.

SEVEN

Stock Footage Production Process Overview

THERE ARE THREE PARTS THAT make up the stock footage production process: preproduction, field production, and postproduction. Let's start with a brief overview of each piece of the production process before going into a more in-depth description.

All three of the processes are necessary, but in my opinion preproduction is by far the most important. As the name implies, preproduction, is the time spent before the production, or shooting, begins. This stage includes storyboarding, auditioning talent, hiring talent, securing the location and sets, building and prepping a set, gathering a crew, securing and testing your equipment, and anything else that should be done before you actually shoot.

During Field production, you implement your preproduction plan. This is when you bring your team, equipment, and talent together to create the footage you will be selling. It is also the most stressful part of the production process. Even though you will have a well-thought-out preproduction plan, the field production process will undoubtedly present you with some unique challenges that you will have to navigate during your shoot.

Postproduction is anything and everything involved after the shooting is completed: editing, color grading, noise reduction, logo removal, and effects, as well as the administrative tasks, including keywording, uploading, and lightboxing that are part of the process in submitting to stock footage agencies.

PRODUCTION IS A LIVING ORGANISM

Another very, very important point to make is that stock footage, for all intents and purposes, is a living organism. Here's what I mean by this. As you're reading this book, you're thinking about what your next series of stock footage uploads is going to look like. You're thinking about the look of the talent and location. You're thinking about wardrobe and props. You're thinking about composition and color palates. (And hopefully, you're thinking about that large number under the "downloads" column.) That's great, and it's important to start with that ideal picture of what you want to produce. But keep in mind that as soon as you get into preproduction, the reality of what you will be able to plan on shooting is going to change, either intentionally, or unintentionally.

After all of your preplanning and coordinating, once you've moved into the production phase, your shoot is probably going to change again because of any number of variables. Your talent might not look as good in person as they did in their pictures. Your location may prove to be less visually interesting than you anticipated. The weather may not be nearly as nice as you had planned. On the flip side, you may have an opportunity to shoot footage that you never dreamed possible. Maybe your location is more amazing than you ever could have dreamed of. Or your talent is able to give you emotional expressions like you could have never imagined. You may even get an opportunity to shoot things that just-so-happen to occur while you're on set.

By the time you reach postproduction, your project has surely evolved even further from where you started. Maybe the number of clips you thought you'd end up with is different because you weren't able to capture enough raw material. Maybe the type and the length of the clips you had anticipated shooting is different. Perhaps after the color grading process you're able to use more of the footage than you originally thought. Maybe you even decide to add some effects to your footage, which you hadn't thought of doing before the shoot. Bottom line is, your production will evolve. Keep this in mind and get comfortable with the fact that it is a living organism, and it will change as you move through the production process.

> DO EVERYTHING IN YOUR POWER TO KEEP THINGS MOVING

From Athens to Upload: A Case Study

A perfect example of "production as a living organism" happened recently during a trip I made to Greece. I went to Athens for an unrelated business conference, and I decided it would be fun to shoot for a half-day while I was abroad and see what kind of footage I could get on the fly. The Uberstock team did a bit of research on my behalf, looking into potential subjects that I could reasonably shoot on my own, versus what was already available in the stock footage market. From that research I identified a few niches that I could target, then I narrowed it down to what I thought would sell the best. Uberstock contacted a talent agency in Greece and got me lined up with a young couple for the shoot. The day before the shoot, I scouted an area around the Acropolis and found all kinds of interesting streets, shops, vendors, artists, architecture, and of course, historical monuments and ruins.

Based on the location scout and my online research, I put together a comprehensive shot list of 72 different shots I wanted to get, everything from simple portraits, to having drinks at a café, to taking selfie pictures from a peak overlooking Athens.

I was pleasantly surprised when on the day of the shoot, the talent looked almost identical to the pictures we had been emailed. Hey, I thought to myself, I might actually get to shoot the *exact* footage I had planned on shooting.

After asking to see the wardrobe options they had brought for the shoot, however, I realized that might not be the case. The man (Paris was his name) brought some great options with no logos (awesome!). Efi, the woman, however, completely missed the mark with her wardrobe due to a miss-communication between me and the agency (oh… the importance of communication during preproduction). Her wardrobe missed so much, in fact, that I had to walk with her to a number of small boutique clothing stores near our rendezvous point to find and buy an outfit that would work. Fortunately, we were able to find a simple yellow dress that fit the bill.

Having averted what could have been a significant crisis, I then inquired about their comfort with showing on-camera affection. Now, keep in mind, like most hired talent, they had only just met. But my vision for the scene was a happy couple traveling in Greece, so my shot list included a few passionate kisses in front of these amazing backdrops, like the Acropolis at sunset. Paris was fine with the kissing; Efi, however, was not so keen.

My heart sank. I was immediately aware that this would eliminate a number of shots that I had not only really wanted to shoot but also had immense potential to be great sellers. Realizing that it would do no good to dwell on what I could no longer shoot, I decided instead to focus on what I could.

I probed further and determined that even though Efi wasn't comfortable with any sort of passionate embrace or kissing on the lips, she was okay with light displays of affection and kisses on the cheek. With this workable compromise, I made a mental adjustment and we got to work. Due to a lack of actual acting experience, some of the shots I had planned on capturing ended up being just plain awkward. In fact, some of the footage was unusable. But, this is why I like to give talent simple, real, actual things to do, rather than asking them to act anything out. In this way, I was able to capture quite a few clips that not only looked great but also felt authentically fun.

The first location was good, but there were more tourists wandering around in the background than I had seen during my location scout. I made a spur of the moment change to my shot list once again. My third location was better. I paid a street artist to draw a portrait of the talent and asked if he would be willing to sign a release as well. He agreed to both. I captured footage of the couple, the artist, the artwork, and reactions between all of them with different focal lengths and from different angles. And because I didn't ask them to do anything other than enjoy the moment (no acting), I got footage that felt much more authentic and usable.

Some of the best results I got were from when I rented a pedal car and asked the couple to ride around the street enjoying each other's company. I gave them direction on where to go and at what speed to travel, but other than that, I didn't ask them to do any acting. Based on the requirements of my shot list, I ran with the camera in-front of them, behind them, and beside them. I shot on both a telephoto lens and on a wide-angle lens. During the forty-five minutes of shooting this particular scene, I was able to capture quite a few fun and great looking clips.

After the pedal car, we started walking the streets around the neighborhood near the Acropolis. Again, due to the crowds, I worked hard to keep my depth of field as shallow as possible by sticking primarily with a telephoto lens and keeping my aperture wide open. I was able to capture a handful of shots of the couple walking along the street from a number of different angles and in a number of different locations. I also asked them to stop for portraits at certain places that I felt were especially scenic. And when we stumbled upon a cozy café with chairs and a table lit by a gorgeous, reflected soft light source through an open window, I couldn't help but to stop and shoot.

It wasn't the outdoor café I had originally planned for a stop, but I went with it. After asking the owner for permission, I shot a number of different establishing shots, two-shots, closeups and cut-aways of the couple's hands and their drinks. In the 30 minutes we were there, I got quite a few shots that I felt really good about.

After the café, we kept moving. We stopped at a few places to shoot portraits, and I captured more footage of them among different backdrops walking hand-in-hand.

But because I got so wrapped up in the visual opportunities of the moment, I neglected to review my shot list with enough frequency to keep us moving with sufficient speed. The setting was beautiful, and I was having a ton of fun. I was in the zone, but I was off track in both my timing and my targeted shot list. As such, I wound up spending way too much time shooting footage that wasn't really that different, and didn't correspond very accurately to what I had planned on shooting. When I did finally stop to look at my shot list and check the time, I realized that the Acropolis was going to be closing in a little over an hour and we still had at least a twenty-minute walk to get there.

Because of this lack of time management, we had to skip three additional locations I wanted to visit and head straight to the Acropolis to get the footage I felt was the most important to shoot.

At the Acropolis, I was much more deliberate in capturing shots from my list. I got about two thirds of the way through my Acropolis list before we were approached by the park ranger and told that the park was closing—a full twenty minutes before the posted closing time. I still had a number of shots I wanted to get and begged with the ranger but to no avail. With nearly thirty minutes of golden hour sunlight left, I took Paris and Efi just outside the park to another peak, loaded with sightseers watching the sun set over Athens. We found a spot where I could compose a handful of shots that allowed us to frame the sunset and avoid any recognizable faces. After shooting a number of different compositions, we wrapped the shoot and headed back to our starting point, where I shared some of the clips with Paris and Efi so they could see the results of their time and effort. (Talent always likes to see their work.)

Feeling pretty good about the day, I got back to the hotel and immediately backed up the footage to three different locations. In a little over four hours, I had shot 190 clips that totaled fifty-seven minutes of footage. I glanced through the clips to look at what I was able to capture that was both a part of, and in addition to, the shot list and found that of the seventy-two shots I wanted to shoot from my list, I really only captured thirty-two of them. So, while I didn't get *most* of what I had hoped to, I also got a ton of footage I wasn't planning on acquiring.

After I got back to the studio, the footage was offloaded and the postproduction process initiated. Footage with recognizable faces in the background was cut. Footage that was slightly out of focus was trashed. Shots were I jostled the monopod were dumped. And shots with multiple takes were culled and consolidated. Over the six hours of editing that transpired, the 190 clips and fifty-seven minutes of footage from Athens was processed into eighty-two different stock footage clips, ranging in duration from five to twenty-nine seconds.

After the edit, the footage was further processed. Some of the shots that were hand-held were stabilized, while others with too much shake were dumped. A handful of clips with visible logos were trashed, while a couple of others were tracked and rotoscoped to erase the offending visual. In a couple of clips, we added a slight blur to background faces that we thought were a bit too recognizable. After all of the fixes were made that we felt were worth making, we put the remaining fifty-nine clips through a color grade and de-noising pass.

Once the final compression and processing were done, we uploaded a total of fifty-eight clips from the Athens shoot. Of these clips, only twenty-seven were on my original shot list. The remaining thirty-one were shots I was able to capture as a result of being both prepared and open to shooting footage I felt could sell while I had the location, time and talent to shoot. (Normally, I'd want to see a bit better ratio of planned versus spontaneous acquisition. And usually, it is more even.)

Efi and Paris in front of the Acropolis, looking more comfortable with our compromise.

Often times, we'll capture ninety percent of what we planned and shoot very little, if any, spontaneous footage. And, in an ideal world, this is exactly what happens: We research the market, scout our location and talent, plan the shoot, author a shot list, and capture exactly what we planned. It almost never, however, goes as planned. That's why I call every stock shoot a living organism. Plan for the best. Prepare for anything. Be ready and open to capturing more than you thought you would, and be okay with the fact that you won't be able to shoot everything you want. This is the reality of stock footage production, and if you're going to produce and make money, it's a reality you'll have to get comfortable with.

EIGHT

Sharpen the Axe (Preproduction)

JUST AS LINCOLN'S SHARP AXE will make quick work of a small tree, so too will thorough preproduction make quick work of a stock footage production campaign. It's not just important. It's critical to your initial and continued success in stock footage production.

There are instances when I'm traveling that I'm not able to follow my standard preproduction process. But whenever possible, I use this simple eleven-step preproduction process in our shoots:

> ### ELEVEN-STEP PREPRODUCTION PROCESS
> 1. Research your market
> 2. Write your stock brief
> 3. Create your budget
> 4. Scout your location (if applicable)
> 5. Lock in your crew and gear
> 6. Recruit and cast your talent

> 7. Build your shot list and create your style boards and storyboards
> 8. Plan and schedule your shoot day
> 9. Gather and prep your wardrobe and props (if applicable)
> 10. Create and send your call sheet
> 11. Prep your gear

RESEARCH THE MARKET

The very first questions you should ask yourself when wanting to create a stock shoot are: What kind of stock shoot should I do? Should I begin with something short? Or am I looking to capture a variety of clips that tell a broader story? Also, what is selling now? And what do I think will continue to sell well in the future? **You must never forget the marketability of the images you are contemplating**—is it compelling enough to garner you a return on the investment that you are putting into it?

Again, it helps to find your place in stock footage *by doing what you do best, and what you love*. If you play to your sweet spot, you will be less likely to go too far afield. Some videographers stray from this "sweet spot" ideal when trying to shoot exactly what a footage agency wants or only what they think the market needs. And more often than not, they don't capture footage that has much market appeal. By all means, you should experiment and try different styles, but don't force what is foreign to your talent, competency, and style.

Producing good footage that will sell well lies in finding a balance, a harmonious relationship between marketability and fine videography. The creative challenge for you, the stock shooter, is to find a way to breathe life into your own work, making it grow and bloom. Always ask this question: Does this concept appeal to me AND can I bring a unique approach to this subject matter? If the answer is yes, go for it!

Refining Your Thoughts

Once you've decided on something (let's say a sunset time-lapse), you should look at what others have done for two reasons: one, to see how it has been done in the past, and two, to get ideas on how you can put your own spin on it for your library. Do a quick keyword study and see what you are able to find on Shutterstock, Getty Images, iStockphoto, Pond5, or any other stock footage site that tickles your fancy. While I firmly believe that no niche has been entirely filled, there is a good chance you will be able to find an example of what you are planning on shooting for reference.

During your search, you'll probably find a lot of garbage as well as some great work. The elements that make up a good stock video, such as the concept, talent, lighting, direction, camerawork, and editing all must fall neatly into place or the project fails. Find videos that appeal to you and watch them numerous times. Take notes on the camerawork, the composition, and the lighting the first time, then the acting, then the direction, and so on. By breaking down a video into these smaller elements, you are better able to see what was effective and what wasn't. From these notes, you'll be able to better refine how you'll shoot your footage with your own unique spin.

> **FIND VIDEOS THAT APPEAL TO YOU AND WATCH THEM NUMEROUS TIMES.**

Again, you should watch existing clips not to **STEAL** their ideas, but rather to see how others approach the same subject. After watching the other clips, ask yourself how you can improve on the concept. Where did their video go wrong… or right? Critiquing is important; you can learn from others' successes and mistakes. But remember that opinions are free because everyone has one, and everyone is a critic. Instead of just criticizing, think of what you can do differently that will improve on what you've just seen—and lead to higher sales and profitability.

WRITE YOUR STOCK BRIEF

Your stock brief is a document that crystallizes what you are going to shoot, why you are choosing to shoot it, who you are planning to shoot it for, and what resources you'll need to accomplish the shoot. A simple stock brief can simply answer those questions with a few sentences each.

CREATIVE BRIEF

CHRISTMAS AT THE RIVERA'S

Shoot Date:
JANUARY, 2014

Key Emotions:
HAPPINESS, JOY, EXCITEMENT, ANTICIPATION, CALMNESS

Producer:
DAWN WAGNER

Director of Photography:
SETH WHELDEN

Assistant Camera:
NOEL ADAMS

Art Director:
ANDI BIXEL

Grip/Electrician:
SPENCER HADDUCK

WHAT IS THE MAIN IDEA OF THE SHOOT?
Day in the life of Christmas. Following the family from the time they wake up to after they finish opening gifts under the tree.

WHAT IS THE STORY ABOUT?
We start with a shot of a husband waking up his wife by bringing her breakfast in bed. He then crawls into bed with her, and they enjoy coffee and pastries together. Meanwhile we see two sleeping children, a brother and sister, sleeping in another bedroom.

BUDGET:
$2,000

ACTIONS/SHOTS TO CAPTURE WHILE THE STORY UNFOLDS:
-Empty shot of the living room without family
-Videoconference both listening and talking to "grandparents" (30 seconds each)
-Portraits both individual and group in front of the tree and in other parts of the house
-Parents taking photos of children opening gifts with iphone
-Children taking photos of gifts and uploading them onto social media
-Children taking photos of each other and their parents
-Father receiving Google Glass as gift
-Various family members using Google Glass
-Children playing on ipad and laptop

© Uberstock

Example stock brief from past "Christmas" shoot.

SimonKR, the most prolific stock footage producer in the world, uses an eleven-page document that outlines everything from the "Key Concepts" and "Key Emotions" to styling and wardrobe, character archetypes, inspirational images, cost per clip projections, and even a backstory for his talent. He is by far, the best-prepared stock footage producer I've ever met.

For most stock footage producers, however, the following stock brief format serves as a great foundation to develop your shoot. Simply answer the questions with a few short sentences that you will later reference to build out the rest of your preproduction materials.

Questions:	Example Answers:
What is the main concept of the shoot?	Blue-collar, hard-working, "salt of the earth" modern-day lumberjacks
What is the story of the shoot?	A day in the life of a team of lumberjacks, logging timber in the early morning fog on a mountaintop. We show individual team members each performing their individual duties with focus, grit, and determination. We show trees falling, chainsaws cutting, equipment working, and the camaraderie of the team on the landing during break time.
What is the visual mood of the shoot?	Lighting is diffused through the fog and mist, with lens flares as the sun peaks through the clouds. Wide backlit silhouettes, high-key closeups, and evenly lit action shots are all necessary to tell the story. The camera will be moving most of the time. It will feel hand-held but will be controlled in its motion. Most of the footage will be shot at a frame rate of 90fps or greater to help dramatize the action of both hard work and danger.

Questions:	Example Answers:
Who is the intended target buyer of the footage?	Advertising and marketing agencies who want to communicate messages of hard work, teamwork, and determination
What is the location where the shoot will take place?	The Coast Range mountains of Western Oregon
What kind of talent will be required?	Real, authentic loggers
What special props will be needed?	None. The loggers will use their own equipment.
How many clips do we anticipate we will produce?	30 to 40
What is the estimated budget of the shoot?	Depending on whether we can secure an inexpensive location and crew, +/- $3,000.

DEVELOP YOUR BUDGET

When we talk to folks who are initially interested in stock footage, a common question on everyone's mind seems to be how much the project (or video clip) cost to produce. While we have repeatedly made the case that large costs **do not** equal top-selling footage, a detailed budget is the only way to determine how much you spent and if you were able

Sharpen the Axe (Preproduction)

to keep the costs down. Also, you will be able to quickly determine your pay-back time, that is, the amount of time needed before the clip begins to more than pay for itself. This section will deal with a quick discussion of the budgeting and other concerns in the preproduction phase.

We have already discussed how some of our most inexpensive shoots also turned out to be some of our best-selling clips. We've also produced big-budget shoots costing tens of thousands of dollars that have generated amazing returns. That said, big budgets don't necessarily mean big sales. We have spent several thousand dollars on a number of productions (for actors, catering, lighting, and assistants) and seen very little return. All this is to say, as much as possible, you want to be VERY sure that the return you get from your clips is commensurate with the money invested. If you shoot long enough, you're bound to have a stinker shoot. But don't let that discourage you. Take solace in knowing that some of your low-cost shoots will eventually bring in the bucks to make up for the riskier shoots that flop. Create a lightbox (I'll explain lightboxes in chapter thirteen) or otherwise flag the clips from a certain shoot that you had. Over time, you can then look back and see how your six-, nine- and twelve-month return has been.

Simon Krzic (SimonKR), again the most prolific microstock footage producer in the world, uses an extensive financial calculation process to predict a shoots payback time BEFORE he shoots a single frame. He uses the prediction to help him determine his production budget. His goal is to recoup his entire investment of a shoot's costs within one year of shooting. Although not to the level of detail that Simon employs, we use a very similar payback forecast to help us set our budgets. If you are new to stock footage production, you won't have the benefit of historical data to guide you in predicting a payback date. If that's the case, you'll just have to make an educated guess on how well you think your footage might sell and set your budget at a level that is comfortable for you.

Take the time to sit down and determine what each area will cost. By having the word "talent" or "equipment" or "food" on a budgeting sheet, it forces you to think about that line-item cost. Go through every other item in the preproduction section and decide how much each area is going to cost. Once everything has been added to this section, do a subtotal and see if you can trim costs anywhere or whether you need to add money. Luckily, this budget isn't carved in stone because it will change. You'll never be able to know every possible variable that will come into play. The best you can do is head these off at the pass and highlight those areas that might quickly escalate dollars.

Example production budget spreadsheet.

SCOUT YOUR LOCATION

The goal of location scouting is to find a space that provides the best opportunity to create footage that matches the visual look as determined by your creative brief. And while finding a location is relatively easy, determining how to make the most of that location is where the real work is done. With this in mind, let's talk about the process of location scouting.

Undoubtedly, one of the most exciting aspects of a production is seeing the potential location for the first time. With this in mind, when you first show up to a potential location, you should have an immediate and very visceral reaction to the space. You should get a strong sense of whether it will work for what you are trying to shoot. If you walk in and immediately know it isn't right, in MOST cases, you should turn around and leave. If, on the other hand, you get the immediate sense that it's perfect or even, "I think this will work," then you have a bit more investigating to do.

The first thing you're going to want to think about when you're doing your location scout is to check for availability, access and control. You need to have a good understanding of how much time you're going to have available at each space. Talk to whoever is in charge of the space and make sure you have access to the places you want to get during the time you want to get there. You also want to make sure you'll have complete control over the space. Meaning, if you want to turn off some lights, or move a table, you have the authority to do so (within reason, of course). It does you no good to land a prime location, if you're not able to control the lighting and staging of the area to capture the footage you need.

> IT DOES YOU NO GOOD TO LAND A PRIME LOCATION, IF YOU'RE NOT ABLE TO CONTROL THE LIGHTING

Oftentimes you're not going to have full access at certain times of the day. You need to make sure you understand when you can get into certain locations. You're also going to want to take a look at where the light is good, especially if you're going to be using natural daylight. The light in the morning is going to look very different than the light in the afternoon. When scouting, you need to be aware of the time of day in relation to when you will actually be there to shoot your footage.

The next thing you're going to do in your location scout is find your staging area. Now, your staging area is just a spot where can bring all your equipment, cases, briefcase, etc., so it's secure and out of the way. You'll probably leave your briefcase, laptop, and other expensive equipment at your staging area, so it should preferably be a space that you can secure and lock. You're also going to want to find a space with electricity to set up your battery charging and media off-load station. Trust me on this—you don't want to find a place to charge your batteries willy-nilly wherever you're shooting. You'll want to have one location that you know your batteries are charging and your media is off-loading. It saves all kinds of headaches both during the shoot and when it's time to wrap and go home.

THINGS TO REMEMBER:
WHEN SCOUTING A LOCATION

- ☐ Trust your initial gut reaction
- ☐ Check for availability, access, and control
- ☐ Make sure the light is good considering the time of day you're planning to shoot
- ☐ Find a staging area
- ☐ Find your electricity sources
- ☐ Consider restroom facilities

What to Bring

The first thing you definitely want to bring is a camera. You want to shoot stills of everything. If you think something could be useful during your production, go ahead and shoot stills of it. Ideally you'll be using the same camera that you would for your shoot but it doesn't have to be.

Also, by shooting a lot of images, it can help save you a trip back later. For instance, if you can't remember, say, if the lights were tungsten lights or if it was daylight, if you have pictures of that, you'll be able to tell and won't need to make a trip back.

How do you find the right location?

Is it better just to shoot everything in the controlled environment that is familiar to you or do you want to deal with the problems that location shooting might bring? Everything must be weighed carefully to determine which best suits your needs.

> **FURTHER QUESTIONS TO ASK AS YOU SCOUT A LOCATION:**
>
> - Where will the sun be and how will shadows fall?
> - Do you have/need overhead fluorescents or wall-mounted incandescents?
> - Will you need a permit to film at this location?
> - Are you visiting the location at a time and date that will closely match when you will actually SHOOT the footage?

One of the key determinants of making a location the right one is the availability of resources necessary for your shoot to happen. First and foremost is accessibility to power. Can you run AC lines? Do you need a generator, and so on? Decide what you'll need when scouting, not when you're at the shoot.

Preproduction takes more time and can be more important than the actual production phase. If at all possible, use preproduction and location scouting time to work out all your potential problems and ensure you have backup plans ready. I've been promised one thing before on locations scout (or convinced myself of one thing), only to arrive on the shoot to a different story.

> DECIDE WHAT YOU'LL NEED WHEN SCOUTING, NOT WHEN YOU'RE AT THE SHOOT.

That's where contingency plans come in. Be prepared for anything. It seems to be the ultimate rule of stock video production—what you don't prepare for…*that's* what will happen.

A location scout shouldn't be rushed. If you only have five minutes to check out a location, you are wasting everyone's time, including your own. How can you possibly check every facet of an ideal spot without spending enough time there? Walk the entire location and look around. Where's the sun? What about sound or visual obstructions, access to amenities, and so on? People don't need too much, but what isn't there, you may have to bring in, such as restrooms, food, power, etc.

Once you find the best location, go there during the time of day you plan to shoot. Locations can look very different in the morning and the afternoon. Just like moving to a new neighborhood, you want to see who's living on the left and the right and what the traffic is like during different times of day. Will those forty college kids having a party on the left, or the senior citizen high-rise apartment on the right, create problems?

Finally, I've found that, if at all possible, it's important to try and shoot in low-traffic, low-volume areas. People are ALWAYS interested whenever a video camera is around, and extra spectators can be distracting to your crew and your talent. You might find the perfect location, but if it's too crowded, remember that you'll have to put time and energy into crowd control and trying to get your actors to focus on the scene at hand. There is something alluring about a video camera (and even more alluring when you have lighting, sound, and other equipment that you may have rented) and it tends to attract a crowd. The last thing you want to deal with is a lot of onlookers, honking cars and people clamoring over each other trying to see the big Hollywood stars that you DON'T have acting in your scene. Again, keeping it low key and subtle is the best approach.

> WHAT YOU DON'T PREPARE FOR... *THAT'S* WHAT WILL HAPPEN

Scouting for Light

In most instances, when it comes to scouting for light, you want to find a spot that has great available natural daylight. It's a lot easier to utilize good, strong, beautiful daylight and modify that light as necessary, than to do a complete build of a lighting setup. On rare occasions, you may want to build your lighting setup from scratch. If this is the case, then you won't need to scout for light as much as you'll need to make sure you have access to plenty of power.

The other thing you're going to want to think about when it comes to light, especially if it's artificial light, is, do you have control over the light? Do the switches on the wall actually control the lights in the room you want to use? If not, how do you control those fixtures? If so, are they dimmable?

Also, with artificial light, be aware of the type of light in your location. As mentioned earlier, different types of lights have different color temperatures. When doing your location scout, make sure you take plenty of notes and pictures to document the light. That way you'll know what you need to bring to the shoot so you can either augment and enhance what is already there, or eliminate all of the existing light and build your own lighting setup.

Looking for Action

Another important aspect of your location scout it to take the time to visualize the action in the space. Look for your angles and sight lines as you walk around. Take pictures of potential compositions. Think about camera moves and talent staging and blocking. See it in your mind—what are the people doing? How are you going to shoot that action to deliver what was outlined in your creative brief? Take plenty of pictures to help you plan your shoot and develop your shot list after the scout.

LOCK-IN YOUR CREW AND GEAR

Finally, step five in the preproduction process is to lock down your crew and your gear. In regards to equipment, the only thing you REALLY need to shoot stock footage is a camera, media, and batteries. That said, there are a handful of additional items that a serious stock footage producer will always have on a shoot. Namely: camera support (tripods, jibs, sliders, etc.), lights, and lighting modifiers (reflectors and flags).

Basic Gear	Serious Gear
☐ Camera ☐ Batteries ☐ Media	☐ Tripod ☐ Jib ☐ Slider ☐ Lights ☐ Reflectors/flags

Sharpen the Axe (Preproduction)

As important as your equipment, however, is the crew you have helping to *use* that equipment. For a standard Uberstock shoot, we generally have four or five people on the shoot, including a director of photography, a producer, a gaffer and/or grip (or two), and a production assistant. Sometimes, we have a separate director, but oftentimes the DP serves as the director in addition to shooting the footage. There are times, however, when I have to shoot alone. In a perfect world, I would ALWAYS have at least one assistant to help with every shoot. You should find someone who can go with you to help carry equipment, move lights, charge batteries, run last-second errands, and make sure talent release forms get filled out properly. If you can find somebody who has experience, it's a major plus. If you can't, that's okay as long as you find somebody who is both attentive and trustworthy. Having one good assistant can easily double your productivity and, consequently, your sales.

> YOUR TALENT SHOULD BE HEALTHY, HAPPY, FRIENDLY, AND GOOD-LOOKING

CAST YOUR TALENT

As we mentioned in chapter six, sometimes it's just easiest to cast your girlfriend, boyfriend, spouse, brother, mother, uncle, or whoever. But if you're investing all this time and money into producing quality stock footage, the important thing to remember over convenience and frugality is that your talent should be healthy, happy, friendly, and good-looking. It is also important that they can act naturally in front of the camera. Recruiting believable, good-looking, friendly talent, however, can be one of the most challenging aspects of any production. Especially if you don't have the money to invest in a talent agency, which most likely you do not.

We also talked about a number of different ways to find talent in chapter six, but don't limit your search just to those options. In today's social-media-saturated world, networking with friends and family who know someone who might know someone is easier than ever. Try posting a casting call to Facebook, or searching for local film and video groups that might include actors looking for work. Call your local theatres, look for schools nearby with acting programs, try your church, or just start papering the community boards at coffee shops near the university. The point is, you should reach out to as many people as you can, because the bigger the pool you have to choose from, the more options you have to make sure your talent is right for your footage. Take time to meet as many potential actors as you can. If they're not quite right for this role, keep their contact information for later; they just might be perfect for your next shoot. If you can't afford a talent agency, use every opportunity to start building your own network of believable, good-looking, friendly talent.

BUILD YOUR SHOT LIST AND/OR STORYBOARDS

Developing a comprehensive shot list BEFORE you get on set will ensure you won't waste valuable time and money.

A shot list is exactly what it sounds like: a list of shots you want to capture during your stock footage shoot. You want to list each shot along with any pertinent information about the shot. For instance, in our shot lists, I also include:

- The desired focal length
- The desired action of the talent
- The movement of the camera (if applicable)

Prioritize your shot list based on need and efficiency. Basically, start with what you feel is most important, as well as how it fits in the overall flow of the shoot. For instance, if you are shooting a scene with

Sharpen the Axe (Preproduction)

two people talking at a table, you'll want to go ahead and shoot both the medium shot and closeup of one person before you move the camera to shoot the medium shot and closeup of the other person.

Think about your shot list in regards to the areas you're going to be shooting in and the shots you're going to want to get.

STORYBOARD

© Funnelbox

This is a storyboard example from a past outdoor shoot.

Sometimes it also makes sense to create storyboards for your shoot. Storyboards are especially helpful if you want to communicate your visuals to a team ahead of time. They help to get everyone involved on the same page in regards to composition, lighting, and even camera movement. Working through the process of producing storyboards can help the director of photography think clearly about the time and resources needed for each shot and ultimately help improve both the efficiency and quality of the footage captured. Storyboards can be produced as simple stick-figure drawings or professionally illustrated by storyboard artists. There is also software available that allows you to create decent looking storyboards from the comfort of your computer.

PLAN AND CREATE YOUR SCHEDULE

A shooting schedule is a detailed, minute-by-minute, plan of what your production day will look like. It starts with a "call time" (the time people show up at the location) and ends with the "wrap time" (the time people drive away from the location). In addition to the time used actually SHOOTING footage, the shooting schedule should take into account any loading times, lighting and setup time, location moves, lunch, or any other action that will take time from the shoot. It is absolutely imperative that you develop a clear and detailed schedule to drive your production for optimal efficiency.

> **QUITE SIMPLY, WITHOUT A DETAILED SCHEDULE, YOU ARE DEAD**

Quite simply, without a detailed schedule, you are dead. With a stock video production crew waiting in the wings, everything hinges on you scheduling the right task to happen at the correct time. As the producer who is in charge of all things that are happening on the set (and off the set), it falls to you to have a detailed schedule of what ***should*** happen, when it should happen, and the resources needed to ensure that it does happen.

When creating your shooting schedule, the first thing you want to think about is that, as with most things in life, everything you do is going to take about fifty percent longer than you anticipate. If you think you're going to get your first shot done in thirty minutes, plan on it taking forty-five. If you're able to get it done in thirty minutes, you'll have extra time for your next shot. Eventually, one of your shots is going to take longer than you anticipated. It's better to plan for that in your schedule then to have to scramble and make adjustments on the day of the shoot.

> **THINGS TO REMEMBER:**
> **PREPARING THE SCHEDULE**
>
> - Plan for everything to take fifty percent longer than you think
> - Apply your knowledge from the scout
> - Give plenty of time to load in and wrap out
> - Be sure to schedule a break for lunch! *Including yourself!*

When scheduling, you also need to consider what you learned from your location scout. For example, what areas were accessible to you at what time? When was the sun shining in the windows just the right amount? At what time of day was the traffic most minimal near your set? Much of that information will be relevant to your schedule.

It's also important to give yourself plenty of time to load in and wrap out of your location. It generally takes two to three times longer to get in and setup as it does to tear down and wrap out. So, if you're planning on sixty minutes for you to get loaded in and setup for your first shot, you'll probably be able to wrap the entire shoot and get wrapped out in twenty to thirty minutes. And if the doors are going to be locked and alarm turned on at seven o'clock, a good production schedule will help to ensure you're out in time.

Also, make sure to schedule yourself a nice break for lunch. I guarantee, when you are in the heat of the shoot, the day is going to fly. It's going to feel like the quickest day of your life. This makes it doubly important to give yourself a nice break at the midway point in your shoot day. Schedule at least thirty minutes to take a breather and take account of what you've shot in the first half of the day, so you can re-prioritize and readjust your schedule if necessary for the afternoon. (More often than not, I end up readjusting some aspect of my shoot during the second half of the day.) Take it from me, you definitely want to give yourself some time to take a breather, get some food, and readjust your plan for the rest of your shoot day.

GATHER AND PREP YOUR WARDROBE AND PROPS

Based on your creative brief and shot list/storyboards, you'll need to determine your wardrobe and prop needs. Document those items, then go about securing them. There's no secret technique to it. Simply write down your list of needed items, then go and get them. You may already own them. You may be able to borrow them. You may have to buy them. Whatever you do, make sure you take the time to get an accurate list of the items you'll need, then check them off as you secure them.

CREATE AND SEND YOUR CALL SHEET

A call sheet is simply a document you provide everyone who is involved with the shoot so they have a clear understanding of the critical information they need in order to show up on time, at the proper location, and with the appropriate equipment. A professional call sheet would include all the talent and crew along with their call time and contact information, the location name and address, the weather forecast—even the location of the nearest hospital. For a stock shoot, you don't need to do all that.

Sharpen the Axe (Preproduction)

> **THINGS TO REMEMBER:**
> **INFORMATION YOU NEED TO SHARE**
>
> ☐ The names, job roles, and phone numbers of all of the cast and crew
> ☐ The call times for each individual involved in the shoot
> ☐ The name and address of the location where you are shooting
> ☐ An estimated wrap time of the shoot

When you email your call sheet, make sure to be clear that everybody is expected to email or call you back to confirm that they actually received the call sheet. Yes, it has happened. People have failed to read the call sheet, only to show up at the wrong place, or at the wrong time based on a previous conversation or a simple misunderstanding. Make sure people respond to you with an email confirming that they understand where they're supposed to be and when they are supposed to be there.

PREP YOUR GEAR

You want to do this the day before your shoot, and it's very, very important. You do not want to skip this step. Prepping your gear is simply the act of gathering your equipment and setting it up like you're actually going to shoot some footage. The day before your shoot, you should grab your camera, lenses, batteries, media, tripod, and lights, set them up, turn them on, and test everything.

If anything isn't working, you want to learn about it the day before. You don't want to learn about a dead camera the day of the shoot. At the very least, you need a camera that works, and you need plenty of power and media. Everything else you can kind of work around if you have to, but that's why you want to test and prep your equipment the day before. That way you can arrive on the day of the shoot with confidence, knowing that all of your equipment is in good working order.

FALL TO YOUR LEVEL OF PREPARATION

"We do not rise to the level of expectation. We fall to our level of preparation."—Archilochus, Greek soldier and poet

It's important to keep in mind that, no matter how good you are, or how many shoots you've produced, there will always be a wrinkle or challenge that you hadn't planned on. If you've done a thorough job of preparing in preproduction, you'll be able to make a relatively easy pivot to keep things moving in the right direction, rather than allowing that wrinkle to derail your shoot. I can't stress enough the importance of preproduction. Have your documents in order. Have your shot list. Have your schedule. Know your locations. Make sure you're clearly aware of what's coming up. If you're thoroughly prepared, you'll be able to shoot incredible footage no matter what challenge comes your way.

NINE

The Shoot: Follow the Plan, but Be Ready to Adapt

LET'S TALK ABOUT THE DAY of the shoot. First thing you want to do is make sure to show up early. You want to give yourself plenty of time to get your staging area ready and prep your gear. Go ahead and set up your charging station. Get your laptop out and ready to offload your media. Get your coffee. You want to be able to have enough time to do all of these things and not feel rushed. Give yourself a minimum of an hour before call time, maybe even two hours depending on how you feel about the location and situation.

Once you get settled in your staging area, move to the location of your first scene to get things set up. Set up your camera. Set up your lights. The idea is to be entirely ready for your first shot BEFORE your talent shows up. That way, when they arrive, you can focus your attention on them, and not on the technical aspects of the shoot. You want to make your talent as comfortable as possible. Go over their wardrobe. Tell them what the scene is about and how you'll want them to act. Make chitchat and get to know them as a person. This will help you to build rapport with them and help to put them at ease. Ultimately, it will make the shoot much easier to navigate for everyone and will result in much better and more authentic footage.

> # ROBB'S RULES
>
> ### SHOOT DAY
>
> 1. Arrive an hour early minimum
> 2. Setup and get entirely ready *before* your talent shows up
> 3. Chitchat to make your talent comfortable

FOLLOW THE PLAN

When it's time to start shooting, one of your priorities is to get through your shot list. You took the time up-front to figure out what you wanted to shoot and had good reasons for why you wanted to shoot it. Therefore, you need to make it a priority to actually get through your list. This is especially true when your shoot goes exactly as planned, which isn't very often. A part of your shot list should include how long you are going to spend shooting each shot. Pay attention to this list, otherwise, you'll come back with thirty-two takes of the exact same clip, only one of which you can really sell. It's much better to get two or three takes of ten different shots than it is to get thirty takes of one. If you want to maximize your time, effort, and financial return, you need to stay focused and get through your shots.

BE READY TO ADAPT

No matter how much preproduction and planning you do, inevitably there will be times when something goes wrong. And when it does, you need to be ready to make a change. I have many stories about being ready to shoot one thing only to realize that I'd have to shoot something else entirely. It might be a problem with talent, or props, or wardrobe, or location. Maybe even *all four* at once!

Mike Tyson once said that everybody has a plan until they get punched in the mouth. That's going to happen to you. You are going to do your preproduction, you are going to have everything setup exactly how you want, but then things will happen. You will get punched in the mouth. Prepare for it now so you can roll with those punches on your shoot later. Hope for the best, and plan for the worst. Always be ready to adapt when necessary so you can alter the plan and still shoot some great-looking stock footage.

> YOU WILL GET PUNCHED IN THE MOUTH.

AN OUNCE OF PREVENTION

If you've spent a lot of time and money on a bigger budget shoot, the pressure of a time crunch can often make people compromise by settling for less-than-perfect lighting, camerawork, background design, or even acting. Under these circumstances, people often like to say "I can fix it in post," meaning that exposures can be tweaked, backgrounds blurred, logos erased, or compositions readjusted when the video gets into the computer back at the studio.

I don't need to tell you, however, that this is much easier said than done. Your best bet, by far, is to capture footage that is as close to **absolutely perfect** as possible on location. Even if it means you have to spend more time on fewer setups and shoot less coverage of the scene. It is preferable to have a well-lit, well-composed, and well-acted shot with nice camera movement than to have a dozen shots that are subpar and need a lot of work in postproduction. Blurring a logo might seem easy on set, but it can take hours, sometimes even days, in postproduction to make it look good enough for a buyer to consider purchasing the footage. Spend the time to shoot things right. Yes, you want to get a lot of footage on your shoots, but in the stock footage world, producers are rewarded for quality, not for quantity. With this in mind, make sure your quality is up to snuff, and don't worry about pumping out hundreds of clips from a single day of shooting.

CHECK YOUR "TECHNICALS"

Last year, I was shooting some footage of two little girls on a beach in Mexico (they *weren't* my daughters, for a change.) Because of the technique I was using, which involved hanging the camera upside down on a monopod as I walked beside them, I wasn't able to critically check my focus while shooting. Even though I did everything I could to ensure good focus, (including using a wide-angle lens and closing the aperture), I made a mistake in setting the focus too close to the lens. The corresponding footage I captured was lit beautifully, composed perfectly, and the smiling young girls moved flawlessly in the frame. The only problem? It was all slightly out of focus and COMPLETELY unusable. It doesn't matter how great your scene is, how perfect your talent acts, or how flawlessly you move your camera if there is a technical issue with the footage you shoot. If it's out of focus, severely under- or overexposed, has too much grain, or has any number of other technical issues, your footage is completely worthless. Make sure, when you're shooting, that you are capturing technically correct footage. Your portfolio and your bank account will thank you.

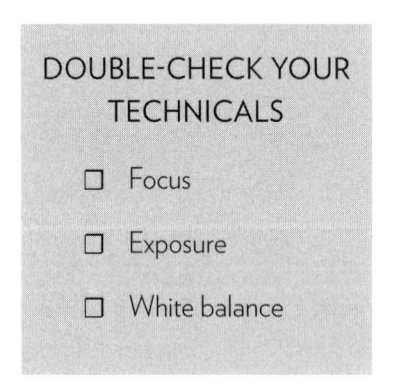

> **DOUBLE-CHECK YOUR TECHNICALS**
> ☐ Focus
> ☐ Exposure
> ☐ White balance

TEN

Shooting With Purpose

WHEN SHOOTING STOCK FOOTAGE, YOU always want to keep in mind what your potential buyer is looking to communicate. As such, you want to be very deliberate when you shoot and do everything possible to direct a viewer's attention to the points of interest in the frame on which you want them to focus.

Being able to intentionally guide a viewer's attention in the frame is one of the true marks of an exceptional stock videographer. A quick scan through the stock footage libraries and you can see that there are far too many sub-par clips from videographers who don't yet understand how to frame their subject, guide their camera to move with the talent, or, who simply setup their tripod without careful thought to how it will appear once their footage is captured. What it all comes down to is intentionality of focal points in your footage.

CONTROLLING THE FOCUS

We've found that our top-selling clips are consistently those that have a simple, clear, arresting center of interest. If a viewer's eyes don't know where to go in a clip or in a frame, there is a sense of confusion in the subconscious of that viewer. In the absence of this center, the eye wanders to secondary areas of the frame, looking for meaning and focus. That's why it is so important to have a strong sense of focus for each and every clip you produce. How you compose, light, and employ movement in your shots is critically important in controlling the focus of your viewers.

> **KEYS FOR CONTROLLING FOCUS**
> 1. Composition
> 2. Lighting
> 3. Motion

With this control of focus idea, there are three technical keys to shooting stock footage that will generate a great return. Those are: composition, lighting, and motion.

COMPOSITION: THE ART OF FRAMING THE ACTION

Composition is one of the most important creative variables of a clip. It is simply defining the position, arrangement, and view of the objects within the frame. When composing a shot, you should keep in mind that your composition is, in effect, representing the point of view of a viewer. And how you compose your shot is going to have a direct impact on how that viewer feels when they see it.

Placing your subject in the top corner of the frame, will evoke a different feeling from your viewer than if you place your subject smack dab in the middle of that same frame. Composing a shot with plenty of negative space in front of your subject communicates a much different feeling

Shooting With Purpose

© Robb Crocker
A composition like this might communicate a sense of "uneasiness" or "claustrophobia" to a viewer.

© Robb Crocker
Unless done for a very specific creative reason, a composition like this might communicate a sense of indifference or boredom.

© Robb Crocker
This is a more traditional and "comfortable" composition. The negative space in this image "feels right" to viewers because it is in front of where the model is looking.

Crowding the subject into the corner and chopping him off at the shoulders feels "awkward" and "uneasy" to most viewers.

than if you crowd your subject into the corner of the frame. Shooting your subject from an extremely low angle is going to affect a viewer much differently than if the shot's from a high-angle position. And leaving a bright light in one corner of the frame might unintentionally draw attention away from the primary focus of your shot. Quite simply, how you frame your subject and the other visible objects around it, and where you place your camera to achieve that framing, suggests something very important to your viewer. It's imperative that you compose each of your shots intentionally rather than haphazardly. This is the kind of thoughtful detail buyers are looking for in the stock footage they purchase.

So, let's talk about the FIVE key concepts to understand in regards to composition: scale, angle, space, background, and color.

FIVE KEY CONCEPTS TO COMPOSITION

1. Scale
2. Angle
3. Space
4. Background
5. Color

Let's Start First With Scale

Scale is essentially the size of the objects in the frame. For the sake of simplicity, we'll use an average female actor as an example. If our camera were equipped with a telephoto lens, the female subject would fill up a large portion of our frame. This would be considered a "closeup." If, on the other hand, we were using a wide-angle lens, our subject would appear relatively small in the frame. This would be considered a "wide shot." You can control the scale of your subject by either moving the camera closer or farther away from it, or by using different lens focal lengths on your camera. There are a number of reasons to change the scale of your subject. Some help to convey emotions. For instance, a closeup shot can convey a sense of intimacy with your subject. A wide shot, conversely, might convey a sense of loneliness. If you're shooting machinery, however, using a closeup might allow you to show the details of the controls, while a wide shot might help to convey the simple enormity of the machine.

LENS OPERATION GREATLY AFFECTS SUBJECT SCALE

Lenses enable you to see the world from any perspective, so it's important to understand how to make the most of them. For instance, we've all seen closeup images shot with a wide-angle lens. It's like looking at someone through the little eyehole on your front door. Features are exaggerated as the camera or person moves closer. Long noses seem to bend around the frame and you see a lot more than what you might want to. A wide-angle lens, when moved in close, is great for humor or for use in playful scenes, like a child's birthday party or a goofy looking actor pulling off a fantastic face or stunt. I have quite a few playful clips that continue to sell well, everything from an Elvis impersonator to dancing Halloween- and Christmas-themed videos.

A good rule of thumb when it comes to lenses is that wide angles tend to characterize editorial footage—you often get a broad view, the whole picture with lots of information in both foreground and background. This is partly due to historical tendencies as well as the practicality of just setting up a camera and letting it roll to capture essential elements in the scene. In high-end advertising, there is often a preference for footage that looks more cinematic. Longer focal lengths tend to be more sought after, often with the background out of focus. Shots with this type of feel tend to lend themselves more to storytelling and conveying emotion.

> SHOTS WITH THIS TYPE OF FEEL TEND TO LEND THEMSELVES MORE TO STORYTELLING AND CONVEYING EMOTION.

A wide-angle lens often will tend to accelerate motion. Several sporting events, such as, car races, are shot with a wide lens to make the cars appear to be traveling at a higher rate of speed. Shooting wide from below gives the illusion of power and dominance (the good guy shot from below, tall buildings looking more ominous, and so on).

The opposite is true with a telephoto lens. Any long lens will compress the image. Through a telephoto lens, even though an actor may be traveling a great distance, the magnification and compression of the lens will make it look as if little distance is covered. Traffic jams are usually shot in telephoto because it makes them seem more congested, and the magnification allows rising heat (and exhaust fumes) to be seen. We've all seen these scenes in various mediums. There are LOTS of ways to show the different messages and themes that are needed.

Anyone with large features can be made to look more flattering with a telephoto lens. These objects are compressed and look more pleasing. The next time you are trying to create a visual image, try experimenting with different wide-angle or telephoto lens' and move the camera accordingly. If used with a great deal of skill and care, you will get the desired effect you're after.

Next Let's Talk Angle

The relationship between the camera and the object being photographed gives emotional information to an audience and guides their judgment about the character or object in the shot. This camera angle is extremely important in both conveying emotion and intent for your shot and helps to direct a viewer's focus.

There are a number of different variables that come into play when determining a camera angle. First, there is camera height. Why does the height of your camera matter? As an example, let's say you're speaking to a small child. When standing facing each other, you are probably looking down on the little tike from above. What you would see would be the kid looking up at you, head tilted back, hair falling, neck exposed. What kind of perspective does that give you as the adult? With this image in mind, if you were to shoot a person at an extremely high angle, looking down on them, your viewer will feel

> **WHY DOES THE HEIGHT OF YOUR CAMERA MATTER?**

superior, and the message conveyed would be one that the subject is inferior and weak. Conversely, if you shoot from an extremely low angle and are looking up at them, the viewer will feel inferior, and your subject will appear strong, powerful, and maybe even intimidating. When you look down on a subject, you diminish their power. When you look up at them, they have power over you. The height of your camera is the perspective of the audience. So think about what you're trying to convey in your shot, because the camera height you choose will have an effect on how your audience feels about your subject. Do you want your subject to appear strong and authoritative? Lower the camera just a little bit. Weak and wimpy? Try raising it up. Just be aware that if the camera height is too extreme or obvious, it can distract your viewers from the message. Instead learn to apply camera height more subtly. For instance, you might position your camera just slightly above your subject's eyeline to convey a sense of innocence or maybe confusion. The possibilities are endless. You simply need to decide which type of emotion you want to convey to your viewer, then execute these camera techniques.

© Robb Crocker

Looking down at this girl makes her seem "meek" and "gentle," giving the viewer a feeling of power over her.

© Robb Crocker

A picture of this same girl taken from a low angle makes her now seem "mean" or "aggressive."

In addition to camera height, you also need to be aware of the camera's placement on the axis relative to the front or back of your subject. For instance, if you were to shoot straight on at your talent and have them look directly into the lens of the camera, it would convey a sense of connection between the subject and the viewer. If, on the other hand, you were to shoot your subject from a profile position, at ninety degrees from the front of their face, you would convey a sense of voyeurism, like the viewer is looking at the subject without them knowing they were there. Depending on the talent and subject matter, this can create an uneasy feeling in the viewer. Again, you need to be deliberate in choosing which type of feeling you want to convey through your footage. A great way to do this is by choosing your camera axis carefully.

Angle Variety

A low-cost way to add production value to your shoot is to add plenty of angle varieties. In short, whenever possible, try to shoot from the angles you think will help you sell your video clip. Think through the time and energy you have expended to get the camera, talent, lighting, and equipment there so far—now don't stop until you've exhausted as many conceivable and valuable angles as possible. Planning your camera angles—i.e. shooting from a low, mid- and high perspective AS WELL AS a variety of medium and closeup angles—is the final part in executing a great shoot. Several different camera perspectives will create variations in emotion and feeling, even when there are no other changes in composition or lighting. Make sure you maximize all shooting opportunities, and be sure you plan for these extra angles. They help to spice up the traditional footage that stock footage buyers are tired of seeing.

The final benefit of having several other angles is that when you start editing, you can feel backed-up, in that there are several takes of the same scene each conveying different feelings and emotions. Archiving a few extra gigabytes of video can pay for itself several times over. So make sure to shoot multiple angles.

Camera angles and shot composition are important tools for visually telling your story in any stock video clip. The way you choose to use them is another part of your personal directing style.

Term	Description
Closeups (CU)	The lens is zoomed in tight on a specific area of the subject, such as the face. Useful for relating details.
Extreme closeup (ECU)	An even closer shot (i.e. the eyes). I have done several portrait-style ECU with some of my favorite subject matters, and these have sold quite well.
Medium shots	Provide a wider perspective of the subject relative to the setting with the emphasis still on the subject (i.e. a shot of an actor from head to toe). This is useful in showing relationships between subject and setting and, if you have invested quite some time in selecting and building the scene, will ensure that you film it adequately.
Two-shots and group shots	Based on medium shots but composed in relationship to the total number of key people in the frame.

Term	Description
Wide shots	Prominently highlight the setting with the subject being relatively small, if at all present in the frame.
Over the shoulder (OTS)	Subject-framed with a portion of another subject's body in the foreground. These are particularly useful for establishing relationships between people as they talk to each other.
Point of view (POV)	Using the camera to represent an event as seen from the perspective of someone present in the scene.

Subject Placement

Subject placement is exactly what it sounds like: Where in the frame is the subject or point of focus placed? Once again, where a subject is placed can have a significant impact on the message that clip conveys. Clearly, a subject can be placed in any number of positions in a frame. That said, there are some standard framing conventions that we want to cover.

CENTERED, RULE OF THIRDS, AND SOMETHING ELSE ENTIRELY

As a general rule, a centered composition is thought to be one of the least desirable types of compositions for cinematic productions. Watch most movies and TV shows today, and you'll rarely see a DP center his subject right in the middle of the frame. A centered composition feels safe and, some would say, boring. A lot of stock footage is shot this way,

STOCK FOOTAGE MILLIONAIRE

© Uberstock
Notice the eyes on the main subject are almost right in line with one of the "pleasing" intersections in the rule of thirds cross-hairs.

© Uberstock
Both the subject's faces and hands are in alignment with the rule of thirds.

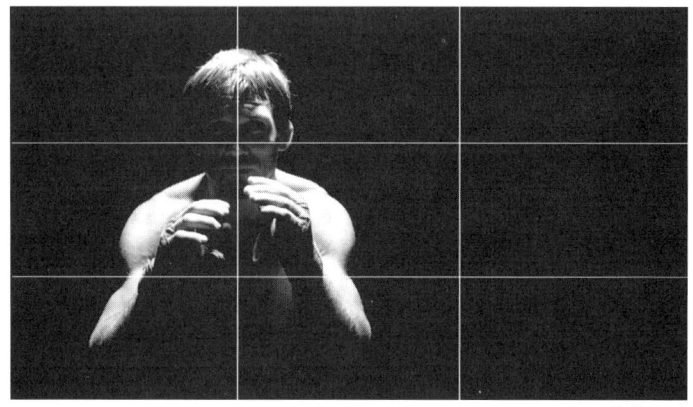

© Uberstock
This fighter is framed to take advantage of the rule of thirds placement.

with a subject centered in the frame. If safe is what you are trying to produce in your footage, then by all means shoot it centered.

If you were to picture a 16:9 frame and imagine that it were divided in thirds horizontally and in thirds vertically, you would have a visual representation of the "rule of thirds." The four places in that frame where the lines intersect are considered pleasing locations to place your primary subject in the frame. Pleasing is a bit subjective, but the general consensus across cultures is that this form of balance tends to be pleasant to the eye, whether it be a frame in a moving picture, a photo, painting, graphic, or even element of architecture.

In addition to framing your subject centered or by using the rule of thirds, there are again an infinite number of ways you can frame your shots that don't fit neatly within one of these two definitions. With this in mind, you should experiment with your own unique framing from time to time. Who knows, that unique take on an otherwise unremarkable shot just might be the trick you need to turn an average seller in to a hot seller.

NEGATIVE SPACE

Negative space is the area that surrounds the main subject in your video clip and is another consideration you'll want to take into account when you are framing your shot. Negative space defines and emphasizes the main subject of your footage, drawing your eye to it. It provides breathing room, giving your eyes somewhere to rest and preventing the visuals from appearing too cluttered. All of this adds up to a more engaging composition.

An additional benefit to shooting with negative space in mind is aimed at your buyers. It's important to remember that buyers are often purchasing your clips to sell something. With this in mind, it often makes sense to give them some negative space so they'll have room for a product photo, graphic element, or on-screen text. You don't want to shoot ALL of your footage with negative space, but you should at least be aware of this need and provide clips that meet this objective as part of your library. If the footage buyer can't imagine his product or logo being placed somewhere in the frame, he will be more prone to find one that allows them this flexibility.

© Robb Crocker

There is plenty of negative space around this clip, which gives editors plenty of room to add additional visuals if necessary.

Background & Foreground

Background and foreground elements are both important pieces to your footage acquisition. A great background can add character, depth, and credibility to your shot and help to make it a top seller. A crappy background, on the other hand, can literally ruin what would otherwise be a great stock footage clip. In the same vein, well-placed foreground elements and action can add depth, texture, and a sense of realism to your footage, while annoying, obtrusive, or poorly conceived foreground elements can do exactly the opposite.

BACKGROUND

As a general rule of thumb, backgrounds should be clean, simple, and clear of distractions. It's called background for a reason, and unless you are working to create a deliberate environment through the use of a specific background, it's usually best to keep it as clean as possible. Background distractions are not just hard to digest aesthetically but will also diminish the profitability of the clip you are working so hard to sell. With this in mind, whenever possible, you should be deliberate in eliminating any and all background distractions before you roll a single frame of footage.

ROBB'S RULES

REGARDING BACKGROUNDS

1. Make them clean, simple, clear of distractions
2. Pleasant visually, but also unobtrusive
3. Watch out for mergers!

Once the distractions are removed from the clips, focus next on what a good background should be: an unobtrusive, but still pleasant visual canvas that supports and pushes attention towards the main subject of the clip. Whenever possible, make sure it's easy for a viewer's eye to flow naturally from the background to the main subject, contrasting him or her or it with the background. Lighting can also help separate your subject from the background, but color, pattern, and motion are important factors to consider.

Also keep an eye out for any silly or distracting mergers. A merger happens when your subject stands in front of an object in the background that suddenly looks like it's become a part of the subject. For example, a lamppost in the background might look like an antenna growing out of your subject's head if the two are aligned that way on camera. Or a rack of antlers on the back wall could make your child actor look like a deer in headlights, literally. They're easy mistakes to make, but ones that can be devastating to the message you're trying to convey.

FOREGROUNDS

Whenever I shoot footage that needs to feel authentic or like it is truly capturing a slice of life, I try to integrate some sort of foreground elements between the camera and my subject. In real life, there is a constant stream of people, machines, and other moving objects that pass through our field of view. Many of these partially and temporarily obstruct our vision. It's what happens. It's real. With this in mind, I like to allow and often intentionally move people and things through the foreground of the footage I shoot. Doing so adds a sense of authentic realism to that footage, and I use that technique when that is the feel I'm trying to achieve. For any number of reasons, most producers are afraid to experiment with foreground elements. That is reason enough for me to employ them quite liberally. If authenticity is what you're after in your footage, I might suggest you do the same.

© Uberstock

By incorporating the counter and the fruit in the foreground of this shot, the viewer really feels like they're standing in a kitchen looking out at this family. In this way, the foreground helps establish place and authenticity.

CONTROLLING YOUR BACKGROUND THROUGH DEPTH OF FIELD

Besides background color, pattern, and placement, there are additional ways to separate your subject from the background. Focus and depth of field are also great techniques for putting emphasis on your subject. With the right equipment and/or distance, you can use the aperture of the camera to essentially blur out the background. This gives the viewer's attention nowhere else to go but to your subject.

© Robb Crocker
A 35mm lens and f11 aperture setting result in a relatively sharp background.

© Robb Crocker
A 70mm lens and f3.5 aperture setting make for a blurred background and force viewer's attention to the main subject.

By varying the lens' focal length (the measurement, in millimeters, from the optical center of a camera's lens to the surface of the camera's sensor) and aperture settings (f-stops), you are able to manipulate the depth of field. A short focal length and narrow aperture will result in a wide depth of field (almost everything will appear in focus), while a long focal length and wide aperture opening will cause a shallow depth of field (only a small sliver of z-space will be in focus). These variations can be used creatively to help you set the mood and tone of the clip you are looking to produce. Wide depths of field allow background objects to be in focus along with the foreground objects. This can work to your advantage by allowing the actors more range to move about during a shot, which is especially beneficial if there is a lot of movement and you're controlling the focus.

A wide depth of field draws attention to details in the background. Or, more accurately, doesn't divert attention from the background. When used properly, a wide depth of field can be desirable, allowing you to fully capitalize on the look of the environment you are shooting in. Obviously, you'd only want this if you had a background and environment that added to the feel and authenticity of the footage. Conversely, if you have a poor or even mediocre background, it makes sense to keep the depth of field in a narrow range, so you can ensure the viewer's focus is literally on the subject that's in focus.

> **A SHALLOW DEPTH OF FIELD IS CONSIDERED MORE CINEMATIC**

There are some shortcomings of the wide depth of field. The additional effort needed to find or create a great-looking background aside, a wide depth of field also requires more light than under normal circumstances because of the smaller aperture settings required.

Because of these disadvantages, many videographers only use wide depths of field when absolutely necessary or for a specific effect. Most, myself included, choose instead to use shallow depths of field that blur the background. An additional benefit of using a shallower depth of field is the feeling that is produced in the footage. It's generally accepted that a shallow depth of field is considered more cinematic in quality and feel, which I believe leads to increased sales and profitability of your footage.

The Final Pieces of the Composition Puzzle are Color & Contrast

The impact of a striking color or interesting contrast in a clip can prove to be a truly significant factor in many top-selling stock images—both moving and still. Color attracts the eye, sets the mood, and can pull a viewer into the scene in a very different way than other components of the clip. And contrast can add sharp and immediate clues to the viewer as to what they should be looking at and what they should be ignoring.

You may be familiar with the research in the field of color and how it creates subliminal associations in the viewer, everything from the uniforms of the employees at your local fast-food restaurant to the tints of web pages and packaging of products. The effective stock video producer lets color affect his clip and understands the evocative nature of color to send clear, strong messages. Conversely, a contradictory or confused use of color will undoubtedly distort the message. The trick is to ensure that the color you are using helps to convey right the message, tone, and emotion.

For example, understanding that reds and warm colors signify love and strength will make them desirable in clips of cozy images of a family by a fire. Also, color today, like so much else in stock footage, takes its cues from much that is happening in the trends and themes of the current advertising backdrop. Again, the latest movies, music videos, Internet videos, and print media will continue to drive much of the latest trends in color. Stay current on the latest images that are being splashed across the pages, monitors, and TV screens around you, then use those social color conventions to communicate feelings and emotion in your own footage.

Contrast can be used as a composition tool in a number of different ways as well. You can add contrast through wardrobe. You can add contrast through the use of a specific background or prop. One of the easiest ways to add contrast, however, is through the use of light. We'll talk more about light later, but you should know that one of the easiest and most effective ways to direct attention is by adding light to certain parts of the frame and eliminating light from other parts of the frame. A simple convention is to make your point of focus brighter than the rest of the image. It not only adds contrast but also is a very basic visual queue (almost like a spotlight) to look at the part of the image that is brightest.

Here is a basic table to help you think about what moods and emotions (both positive and negative) various colors can evoke.

Color	Positive	Negative
Red	love, passion, heat, bravery, stop	war, rage, blood, danger
Yellow	joy, optimism, happiness, gold, riches, glory, power, splendor	cowardice, warning, sickness, quarantine, jaundice
Blue	relaxation, trust, integrity, success, water, escape	sadness, melancholy, depression, cool
Green	health, growth, revival, rebirth	envy, jealousy, sickness

Color	Positive	Negative
Black	sophistication, chic, elegance, power	death, mourning, evil, fear
White	purity, cleanliness, innocence, light, truth	cowardice, surrender

LIGHTING

Nothing in your frame would exist without light. Light is what makes video possible, and it's the difference between what your audience sees and what they don't see in a frame. We've already talked a lot about lighting in chapter four, but know that as far as composition goes, light can direct a viewer's attention around your frame more effectively than almost any other technique you could master, accept for maybe shallow focus. Whether it's the intensity of the light that you shine on your subject or the contrast between the amount of light on the subject and the absence of light in the background, there are a number of ways in which you can influence an audience's attention using light.

The color and shape of the light you use are also capable of directing attention. Say you're shooting at night on a city street, with a yellow key light pointed at a man creeping through an alleyway. Say you also point a red key light at the dumpster behind him, revealing a person's arm hanging out. Your attention might be on the man because he's the one moving in the frame, looking creepy, but that red light also draws our attention to the arm in the dumpster, which makes this scene dramatically more telling. Now the man stops in the frame under a dappled light, we assume from a broken street lamp or maybe even an overcast moon, and the uneven light creates shadows on his face that make him look terribly sinister. That's using light to help tell a story in your footage more effectively.

MOTION

I firmly believe that mastering the art of movement in stock footage production is key to separating average stock footage producers from the top-selling producers. Moving subjects in the frame and moving your camera to create dynamic framing creates footage that communicates an authentic story and conveys a message that buyers are looking to utilize. We'll take some time to talk about the two ways to add motion to your footage, namely, movement in the frame and movement of the frame.

Movement In the Frame

In technical terms, this is called blocking. It's how things move in and around the framed image, and it's critical to your message. So think about the action in your shot ahead of time. How can those actions help communicate your idea, feeling, or emotion?

For example, say we're shooting a woman, kind of frantic and in a hurry, flagging down a taxicab on a city street. Visually speaking, would her energy be better told by a shot where the cab is parked on the side of the street, already stationary in the frame or a cab that races into the frame, stops for her to jump in, then races out of frame? I would argue the latter.

Movement can help tell your story, but it can also hinder it. When the woman raises her hand to flag down the cab, for instance, where does her hand stop? Is it right in front of her face? That would create a serious disconnect with our audience. Rehearse this movement with your actress ahead of time so she knows to raise her hand just slightly more to the left or the right so we see her face throughout the entire action. And before the cab comes racing into frame, make sure you and the driver both know where he needs to stop in order to stay in the frame.

Movement of the Frame

When properly motivated, camera movement can be a great tool to use to help convey a feeling, idea, or emotion. Moving the camera creates a sense of depth and gives a viewer some additional perspective of a scene. These elements work to help draw a viewer's attention *into* a shot and communicate a message in a more dynamic and engaging way.

Subtle camera movement allows you to create feelings of openness by revealing more of the scene than was initially perceived. This is especially helpful if you've gone to great lengths to set up the ideal background and staging of your clip. Keep in mind, however, that extreme camera movements can actually prove detrimental to your footage by drawing attention to the camerawork itself, rather than towards your desired point of focus. If not done carefully and with a very deliberate purpose, this extreme movement can unnerve the viewer. They will find it difficult to fix their attention on any particular part of the scene, and thus they will look for someone else's clip to buy. There are a number of ways you can integrate effective camera movement into your footage. Great examples include panning and tilting, dolly moves, crane or jib moves, Steadicam movement, and even simple hand-held movement.

> **THINGS TO REMEMBER:**
> **REGARDING MOVEMENT**
>
> 1. Movement should be motivated
> 2. Practice the move before shooting
> 3. Keep it subtle

Panning and Tilting

One of the primary ways I integrate camera movement into my footage is through simply panning and tilting the camera on a tripod. Of all of the methods available to use, it consistently delivers the nicest-looking movement in the easiest and most efficient manner. When using a professional tripod head, it's easy to adjust the tension and drag settings to help you acquire smooth, fluid camera movements that add a dynamic element to your footage without drawing any attention to the camera move itself. Unless I am specifically looking to lock down a shot, I almost always keep my camera fluid on a tripod head to add a bit of movement and life to my shots.

Dollying

Another fantastic way to add a dynamic motion element to your footage is to use a dolly or slider to move your camera in a straight line on the X or Z axis (side to side or forwards and backwards). It takes a bit longer to set up a dolly or slider move, and you may have to rehearse the move a few times to synchronize any kind of focus adjustment that may be needed. This is especially true if you are moving towards or away from your subject. That said, dolly moves bring with them a certain sense of professionalism and add a ton of perceived production value to your footage. Many of our highest-grossing clips use dolly moves, so we integrate them fairly often when we feel they're warranted by the subject matter.

Jibbing or Craning

If you are interested in adding vertical movement to your footage, more often than not you will be utilizing a jib or crane. Well-executed vertical movement on a shot can feel almost magical, giving the viewers a sense of what it's like to fly. Again, when done with direction and purpose, it adds a TON of production value and can make your footage really stand out in the market. The downsides to using a jib is the amount of time it takes to set up and the amount of skill it takes to effectively execute. Even the simplest jibs can take a minimum of thirty minutes to set up and most will take well over an hour. Add to this a tear down time of roughly half of the setup time, and you can see why there aren't a lot of producers who take the time to use a jib for their footage.

In addition to the time it takes, there is also the execution factor. If you're doing a simple up and down motion with a straight forward reveal of the subject you are moving towards, the execution of a jib move *can be* pretty straightforward. If you start adding panning and tilting to the move, however, or any kind of movement toward or away from your subject, you can add a ton of complexity to your shot. You have to worry not only about operating a remote head for the camera pans and tilts, but you also have to operate a remote focus to ensure what your shooting will actually be usable. With all of these elements in play, you'll have to get help, either someone to operate the jib, someone to operate the remote head, or someone to operate the focus of the camera. If you are inexperienced in operating a jib, you may even need multiple people to help. If you are able to successfully set up and operate a jib, however, with well-executed action and dynamic subject matter, you can really hit a home run in the sales department.

Steadicam

Steadicam is actually the brand name of a camera stabilization system that allows you to walk or otherwise move with a camera while experiencing virtually no visible shake or bounce. There are a number of different systems out there that do the same job of a Steadicam, with different names, Glidecam and FloatCam, to name a couple. Similar to a jib or crane, a camera stabilization system can add incredible production value to your footage. But once again, that value comes at a cost.

> A CAMERA STABILIZATION SYSTEM CAN ADD INCREDIBLE PRODUCTION VALUE TO YOUR FOOTAGE

Properly setting up a camera stabilization system can take a long time—up to an hour or even more. It also takes a lot of practice to learn how to properly operate one. In all honesty, I don't think *any* of the footage in our portfolio was shot with a professional camera stabilization system. This is due to a number of factors. For one, I've become pretty good at minimizing camera shake and bounce even when I'm hand-holding the camera. Additionally, buying, learning, and setting up a professional system can be incredibly expensive and time consuming. There are plenty of other stock footage producers that have invested in and continue to use a professional system, and I'm sure they've found it to be a very valuable tool in the production kit. For me, however, I've never found the potential benefits to be worth the extra time and expense it would take to properly use one.

Hand-Holding

Hand-held shooting can be used to create extreme camera movements or, in the hands of a skilled operator, provide shots comparable to a tripod. Hand-held camerawork is popular for the feeling it elicits by making the stock video buyer feel like a part of the scene. Another benefit is that it is quicker to set up hand-held shots than shots where the camera is mounted on a support system such as a tripod or dolly. However, it's vital that you are very careful with handheld cameras— these should be used deliberately and with a great deal of caution. The risk of shaky, unstable footage is great enough that you need to be very selective.

If you must hand-hold the camera, always hold it away from your body if you are walking or tracking the subject. You will find that your arms and legs, if you walk correctly with your knees bent, will act as shock absorbers to cushion the impact of your movement. We have repeatedly gotten compliments on our stock footage, with folks SURE we used a dolly or steadicam when in fact it was just us walking carefully and slowly through the scene.

> IF YOU MUST HAND-HOLD THE CAMERA

Drones

I'd be remiss if I weren't to at least *mention* the use of drones in stock footage production. Only once have we used a drone to shoot footage. To say it was underwhelming would be an understatement. In hindsight, the subject matter and location weren't ideal, so I don't know that I could honestly say I gave the tool a fair shake. I think the potential for using drones in certain situations could be incredible. But again, it would have to be for the right reasons and in the right situation. They are NOT cheap and take a long time to learn how to operate both safely and effectively. If flying drones is something you are or could be passionate about, then I'd tell you to go for it. That could be an incredible niche that you could capitalize on in the stock footage market. If you weren't fully committed to doing whatever it takes to learn how to do it right, however, I'd caution you against it and encourage you instead to focus on a different method for adding motion to your footage.

DIY Options

In addition to the options I talked about here, there is a limitless supply of DIY solutions. I have used towels dragged on a bar top to move a camera. I have used skateboards and even wheeled garbage cans. One of my favorite methods for moving a camera is even to use a monopod to hang my camera upside down while I walk or run. The point is that there is no limit to the creative ways you can dream up to add camera motion to your footage. Just remember, the key to successfully integrating motion into your footage is to make sure the movement is drawing attention towards your subject or point of focus and not towards the camera movement itself.

A Final Thought on Camera Movement

If you are moving your camera to follow the action of a subject, always give space in the frame for the subject to move into. Keep the subject to one side of the frame, giving them plenty of space to move forward rather than framing them dead center. Again, it feels more comfortable for the viewers and makes your clip more saleable to your buyers.

Term	Description
Panning the camera	Rotating the camera on a horizontal plane (i.e. turning left to right and vice versa)
Tilting the camera	Rotating up and down on a vertical plane. Typically these open the scene up or close out the final frames

Term	Description
Dollying the camera	The camera is mounted on a wheeled device that allows it to physically move across a horizontal plane.
Booming or craning	The camera is up in the air or down using a jib arm or crane. These shots add much sought-after production value to your video clip.

ELEVEN

Taking Care of Business

WITH ALL OF THE TIME and money that goes into preproduction and shooting, you DO NOT want to enter the postproduction phase only to find out that you cannot use your footage because of missing paperwork or malfunctioning equipment. You've got to cover all your bases.

GET YOUR TALENT RELEASES SIGNED

We talked about the need to get talent releases signed in chapter six. This is an important point to reiterate, however. If you don't have a signed release, as far as any stock footage company is concerned, you don't have a clip to sell. It's really that simple. Take care of your release forms BEFORE you shoot ANY footage. Then put them in a VERY safe place. I prefer to have talent release forms filled out and ready to go before the talent even shows up. And when they do show up, the first thing I do after greeting them with a warm smile and handshake is ask them to fill out the release form so they can get paid. (Yes, I pay almost all of my talent, unless it's one of my daughters, in which case it costs me a trip to the local Funland.)

Now, if you're shooting editorial footage, that's a whole different animal—an animal I'm not familiar with and can't talk about with any authority.

BACK UP YOUR ASSETS

Backup your footage immediately. Almost all cameras these days shoot in a digital-file-based format. Remember, after you shoot, the fruits of your labor exist in only one place: a CF card, a hard-drive, or some other media. I have talked a lot about the best way to get your footage in the camera, but you can't stop there. The critical practice of storing, accessing, and managing your archived stock footage is not a place to cut corners. BEFORE you leave the shoot, I always advocate that you BACK up your media. Bring a laptop and some hard-drives, them make sure to back up your footage… twice.

Before even heading out on a shoot, be sure that you have all of the necessary equipment for backing up on the checklist: We use a laptop, a high-speed card reader for data transfer, and two external hard-drives. Double-check that your laptop has enough available hard-drive and memory space to accommodate the amount of footage you're planning to shoot. The file size of your video completely depends on the type of camera you're shooting with and how it encodes the footage. But look this information up ahead of time, because you're also going to want to bring external hard-drives that are big enough to hold all of your footage. It's also important to note that you should invest in *durable* hard-drives. If you're bringing these babies back and forth from your office to the field, they need to hold up. Saving a few bucks on cheap hard-drives can cost you thousands of dollars in lost footage and sales if you're not careful. I also can't stress enough the value of a high-speed card reader for offloading your media footage. Yes, you could skip the reader all together and plug your camera directly into the laptop (given that it has the proper ports), but the files are going to transfer much more slowly and cost you valuable shooting time.

It's important also, to establish and practice an efficient workflow when you're backing up footage during a shoot. Ideally, you'll have so many media cards that you won't have to erase anything while you're under pressure on set. But regardless, think smart and back up as you go. Not after each shot, but definitely as you fill up cards and as time and manpower allow. Pop them into a card reader and let it start transferring over to the drives while you're shooting on your next card.

ROBB'S RULES

YOUR ASSETS

1. Back them up immediately.
2. Make a minimum of TWO copies!
3. Properly eject media, or risk corruption.

When you've finally wrapped the shoot and you've finished backing up, check the information on the drives to make sure the total data size and item numbers match. This is the quickest way to ensure that you've successfully made double copies of everything—double copies in at least two different places. This could be a laptop and an external hard-drive, two separate external hard-drives, the original media cards and a hard-drive, etc. Be sure to properly eject and unplug all media for fear of corrupting your data. Data corruption is a serious beast, and if you're not careful, it can cost you dearly.

TWELVE

Master Your Post

POSTPRODUCTION IS THE CRITICAL PROCESS of turning raw footage into a valuable, revenue-producing asset. If managed well, the postproduction process can quickly and efficiently generate high-quality, download-ready footage. If done poorly, however, it can be a frustrating time-suck of a process that includes editing, rendering, re-editing and re-rendering over and over until you finally get it right. In short, if you don't have a bullet-proof postproduction process, it can be the absolute bane of your existence. With this in mind, let's walk through our nine steps to effective, efficient postproduction.

> **NINE STEPS TO EFFECTIVE, EFFICIENT POSTPRODUCTION**
>
> 1. Back it up, and structure it right.
> 2. Transcode your footage (if applicable)
> 3. Edit pass one: throw out the trash

4. Edit pass two: usable content
5. Edit pass three: the stuff that will sell
6. Quality control: BEFORE you prep
7. Get your fix on (if applicable)
8. Add some FX (if applicable)
9. Do some grading

BACK IT UP, AND STRUCTURE IT RIGHT

There is no worse feeling in the world than shooting a ton of great footage only to have it vaporize because of a bad hard-drive or careless backup and/or archive process. I know this firsthand. Yes, it's incredibly important that you make at least two copies of your media while still at the location of your shoot. But know that it's just as important to make sure you have at least two copies of your media at your postproduction facility as well.

As soon as we get done with a shoot, we offload our footage to a redundant SAN (storage area network) raid that also gets backed up every night. In simpler terms, this is a giant, 12 terabyte hard-drive that backs itself up on the fly and makes another copy to a separate hard-drive every night. Once we're done editing, processing, and uploading our footage, we then take the media off the SAN and make two copies of both the raw footage and edited clips. We keep one copy at our studio, and we take one copy to an off-site location.

As you think about archiving and backing up your footage, it's important to remember that your footage is an asset. It's a piece of property that generates income. You need to make sure you're protecting that asset and your future income.

There are many different ways to set up a backup and archive system. I gave you a brief look at how we structure ours, but this isn't the only way to set up a reliable system. One potential solution might be to take it to the cloud. There are a bunch of fantastic cloud-based storage solutions that would solve the safety and redundancy issues pretty easily. The players are constantly evolving, but it might be worth checking out Dropbox, Google Drive, Amazon Cloud Drive or any other number of cloud-based storage providers. One relatively new player that I really like is Nimia. They offer a service built specifically for video producers, which includes an integrated marketplace for selling stock footage as well. As of this writing, storage for marketable clips is FREE if they are made available for licensing. (If you want to back-up your raw footage for safe keeping, you can pay a small fee to do that as well.) Whatever route you decide to pursue, make sure to take some time BEFORE you shoot to develop your own system. You DO NOT want to suffer the consequences of losing a shoot because of sloppy or inadequate safety precautions. It really sucks. Believe me.

TRANSCODE YOUR FOOTAGE (IF APPLICABLE)

Depending on what file format you shoot your footage in, and what file formats your video editor can handle, you may need to transcode your footage to a different codec. Currently, we shoot our footage primarily in the Red.r3d codec, but also shoot in a compressed h.264 codec, on occasion. When we are processing simply for HD uploads, we immediately transcode the footage to Pro-Res 422 for postproduction. When preparing footage for 4K uploads, however, we process our footage in the native.r3d file format. Whichever file types and codecs you use is really a matter of personal preference, availability, and cost. And as technology continues to improve, new and better codecs and processes will emerge. The simple key is that you need to be thinking ahead of time what, if any, transcoding you will need to do to your raw footage before you start editing. It takes time to crunch those

THE PARTICULAR STRATEGY WE EMPLOY IS TO EDIT IN PHASES.

bits in the computer, and you need to plan for that time in your post-production process.

THE EDIT

The particular strategy we employ is to edit in phases. We do this for a few reasons. Because we have a team that works together in post-production, editing in phases allows us to break up the process into smaller chunks of time, so if one person isn't able to complete postproduction for an entire shoot, they can at least get a portion of the work done and leave it in a place that is easy to sort and understand. It also makes it easy for someone new to pick up the process where it was left off. We also edit in phases for financial reasons. We find that if there is a series of clips that sells particularly well, by editing in phases, we can more easily go back to the raw footage and pull out additional clips that we know weren't a part of the original batch of uploads. This is especially useful, because we don't have to guess whether it was uploaded already because it is in a different track on our editing timeline. Let's talk about the specifics of how we edit in phases.

Phase One: Throw Out the Trash

For the first pass of editing, we simply get rid of the junk. We put ALL of the footage on the V1 track of our editing system. From there, we run through the footage as quickly as possible to cut out all of the stuff that is clearly unusable. Examples of unusable footage might include shots that are out of focus, shots where the talent laughs in the middle of a serious take, or shots where a camera gets bumped or jostled. Basically, anything that we are certain won't sell gets cut. This usually eliminates fifty to sixty percent of the footage. After cutting out the garbage, we then move our usable footage up to track two of our timeline for the next phase.

Phase Two: Usable Content

During the next phase of editing, we slow things down a bit. We look through the usable footage with a more discerning eye to separate the best footage from that which is simply usable. We look for those moments where the camera movement compliments the action on screen, or where the light hits the lens for a perfect flair as our talent smiles at the camera. We look for shots that have a clear sense of focus and communicate a feeling or emotion. Oftentimes that means selecting one particular take of a shot over another that is almost identical. It's part science AND part art. You have to look at the clip from a technical point of view to make sure the exposure is good, the focus is locked in, and the composition is complementary to the subject matter. Also, you have to look at each shot creatively. You have to get a sense for the feeling and/or emotion conveyed and try to put yourself in the shoes of a potential buyer. Ask yourself the question, "Would I purchase this clip, if I needed to communicate a specific message?" If you think the answer might be yes, then move that clip up to track V3 on your timeline for the final step in the editing process.

> ASK YOURSELF THE QUESTION, "WOULD I PURCHASE THIS CLIP, IF I NEEDED TO COMMUNICATE A SPECIFIC MESSAGE?"

Phase Three: Trim to Fit

For the final stage of the editing process, you will lengthen or trim your best clips to meet the time requirements for submission on the stock footage websites to which you'll be uploading. As you trim your footage, you'll want to look at the clips as an editor would. If possible, give the clip some head and tail space for another editor to use. Meaning, if the primary action of your clip is a man running across the screen, make sure you leave at least a second or two of footage before the primary action starts, as well as a second or two of footage after the action is complete. This buffer gives editors options in postproduction, like adding cross-dissolves or fades to a clip without disrupting the main action of the footage. Options are an editor's best friend. If you give your potential buyers that extra head and tail space, it will only make it easier for them to use.

While in the trimming phase, you'll also want to be extremely diligent about the lengths of your clips from a purely technical perspective. If the maximum clip length a stock footage agency will accept is thirty seconds and you upload a clip that is thirty seconds and one frame, the clip will be rejected, and you'll have to spend valuable time fixing what should have been a very easy part of your postproduction process. As a safety precaution, we always keep our clips three frames under the maximum length allowed and add at least three frames to the minimum clip length allowed if we have a shorter clip. I know of other stock footage contributors who also consider this a best practice.

QC—BEFORE YOU PREP

Once you finish your trimming, it's time to take a highly critical look at your footage. When you submit your clips to the stock agencies, there is a real live human on the other end who looks at your work with a VERY critical eye. It's their job to ensure that all of the footage that is being curated into their collection is both creatively strong but also technically acceptable. From a technical standpoint, if you send them files that are full of grain, over-exposed, out of focus, or otherwise less than stellar, they won't accept them into their collection, resulting in disappointment, frustration, and a lot of wasted time and effort on your part. From a practical and/or creative standpoint, they may reject clips because the camera is too shaky, there is no real point of focus in the shot, or simply because the footage is just plain boring. (Ducks on a pond, anyone?) So, before finishing your clips with a color grade, before spending time on compression and uploading, you should act as your own inspector and reject bad clips yourself.

IT'S TIME TO TAKE A HIGHLY CRITICAL LOOK AT YOUR FOOTAGE

From a technical perspective, there are a few things you'll need in order to do that. Mainly, you'll want to have a well-calibrated monitor that is capable of viewing your clips in their native resolution and frame rate. Once you have that handled, you'll want to view your clips specifically for elements that could be cause for rejection. Here are some of the most common objective technical reasons clips get rejected:

- **Focus.** While your clip looks great in the viewer of your camera, or at half resolution in your timeline viewer, it may not look so good at full resolution. Make sure to check for technical focus of your clips.
- **Grain.** If your camera settings weren't optimal and/or the lighting situation of your shoot was less than ideal, your footage might have excessive grain. Again, this is something you need to view in full resolution to check. There are software solutions that can help minimize some grain in your footage, but it can only go so far. If you have excessive grain in your clips, you'll want to save a lot of additional time and effort by tossing them before you upload.
- **Compression artifacts.** Similar to grain, sometimes your footage can succumb to compression artifacts that, while not visible in small viewers, are extremely

visible in full resolution. As with grain, there are some software solutions that may be able to help mitigate a small amount of artifacting, but it definitely has its limits.

- **Exposure issues.** If your clip is severely over- or underexposed, it will get rejected. Most inspectors allow a bit of creative license for certain clips, especially when it comes to slight overexposure. That said, I would highly suggest that you concentrate on uploading properly exposed footage. It's better to be safe than sorry.

- **Logos and bogeys.** If you are shooting royalty free stock footage (which is the subject of this book) then you have to make sure your footage can be sold as such. That means you can't have any visible logos or bogeys (unreleased talent) in your footage. In certain circumstances, there are copyright issues with showing certain types of furniture, cars, and other objects as well that can trigger a rejection. (Although, as long as the objects aren't the center of attention in the shot, it's usually not an issue.) Be ultra diligent about checking your footage for logos or recognizable people in your footage that aren't properly released. This isn't subjective. Your footage WILL be rejected if any of these are present.

- **Off-limit subjects**. There are certain places, landmarks, objects, subjects, brands, trademarks, events, and even *colors* (in certain context) that are straight up off limits on stock sites because they've been identified as having intellectual property infringement issues. This list is extensive and updated frequently, so you should consult your stock agency for the most current information *before shooting*. Just a few random examples include: the American Museum of Natural History, Crazy Horse Memorial, the Hollywood sign, Pike Place Market, 3D interior renderings, burning flags, Frisbees, people's signatures, McDonalds fries (even if the logo is removed, the design of the fry container is copyrighted), Burning Man, Major League sporting events, and the list goes on and on.

From a creative and practical standpoint, there are a number of reasons your footage can be rejected too. Here are some of those that are more common.

- **Camera shake.** If there is excessive camera movement that distracts from the main focal point or subject of your footage, it will probably be rejected. Yes, you can shoot and upload hand-held footage, but it must not distract your viewer.
- **Lack of focus.** This isn't technical focus, but subject focus. Be sure that if someone asks you what your shot is trying to communicate, you have a clear answer. "I don't know," or "I'm not really sure" won't cut it. Make sure you know what you're shooting and why you're shooting it. The inspectors will thank you.
- **Boring or oversaturated content.** If your footage is excessively boring, or if your shot doesn't bring anything new creatively to certain subjects that have already been shot thousands of times by other contributors (like time-lapse clouds), there is a good chance your footage will be rejected. As I mentioned in an earlier chapter, if it's easy to shoot, it's been shot. And if it has been shot enough, the agency won't want to add more, unless it brings a truly unique perspective or form of execution.

GET YOUR FIX ON (IF APPLICABLE)

After reviewing your footage for technical issues, you may find that there is an opportunity to actually fix it in post. Obviously, it takes time (which is money) to fix clips that weren't shot properly. So, if you're going to invest the time to de-grain some footage, or stabilize a shaky shot, make sure you feel confident that the time and effort will be worth it. Basically, if you're going to fix something, you have to truly believe it will result in significant future sales and revenue.

There are a number of different postproduction fixes that can help you save a shot. We'll talk about a number of them here, but know that there may be others you could employ that I won't cover.

THINGS TO REMEMBER:
YOU CAN FIX IT!

- Noise reduction
- Image stabilization
- Exposure compensation
- Logo removal
- Selective blurring
- Add some FX
- Color grading

Noise Reduction

Noise is when your footage looks grainy and, subsequently, cheap. It's the result of insufficient or improper lighting. It takes a lot of time and practice to successfully remove noise in postproduction, but with the proper software it is often (but not always) possible. Noise reduction can be a crucial process for meeting today's high-definition quality standards. Just be aware that there's a trade-off to reducing noise, namely a slight softening of the image. Fine details may get blurry and bright spots tend to smear. I would encourage you to employ noise reduction when needed, but know that it is no substitute for shooting footage with a proper exposure in the first place.

Image Stabilization

Image stabilization is another fix in post that can make your shaky, otherwise unusable footage smooth and steady. Sometimes *slight* camera shake is a style choice that certain people like, but the general rule of thumb for stock footage is to appeal to the largest number of buyers possible. Smooth, steady footage is the most usable kind of footage for the majority of buyers. This is especially applicable as most stock clients are assembling lots of different clips together into one project, so the footage needs to look uniform. As with noise reduction software, image stabilization can work wonders for slightly shaky or unstable footage, but it too comes at a cost. Image stabilization software basically crops your footage then moves the image in direct opposition to how the camera was shaking when the footage was acquired. Because the software has to engage in a digital zoom of your footage, you are in actuality losing resolution when you employ this technique. The more extreme the stabilization, the more resolution you sacrifice. Again, mild stabilization can turn a borderline clip into a money shot. But if used to extremes, it can come at a pretty hefty price on your resolution.

> **APPEAL TO THE LARGEST NUMBER OF BUYERS POSSIBLE**

Exposure Compensation

Exposure compensation is the correction of under- or overexposed areas of your footage. We do some general exposure compensation when we get into color grading. Severe exposure compensation is for when you get footage that isn't easily fixed. If a shot is severely under or overexposed, it may not be salvageable. And, sometimes when pushing exposure compensation to extremes, you end up adding grain, which then becomes another issue. Obviously, it's always best to shoot your footage with a proper exposure. Know, however, that in some instances, you can fix footage that was improperly exposed during a shoot.

Logo Removal

Logo removal and/or blurring are exactly what they sound like. Royalty free stock footage cannot contain any recognizable logos whatsoever (unless, of course they are fake logos you designed for the shoot itself). Sometimes those pervasive little symbols sneak into the shot without you realizing. If they happen to fall on the outer edge of the frame, you might be able to crop them out (albeit at the cost of resolution, which isn't ideal). More advanced techniques include motion tracking, matte framing, and blurring out (or even erasing) the logo in the footage. There's a learning curve here, but in certain circumstances, it can be well worth the effort.

Selective Blurring

Selective blurring, especially on faces, is never ideal, but in some cases it might help you get around missing talent release forms. If a random dude (aka bogey) happened to walk into the background of your shot, you could gently blur his face enough to ensure he has no discernible features. Just make sure that your blurring matte is subtle enough to blend into the background rather than draw the viewer's attention.

ADD FX (OR NOT)

There are times when it might prove beneficial to add a special effect to your footage. There are more than a handful of stock footage producers that utilize chroma keying, particle effects, faux lens flairs, and so on to give their footage that extra something that makes it stand out in a viewer's mind.

© David Baumber

One of Multifocus' most successful clips is a composited clip with live action footage and animation.

David Baumber, better known as Multifocus to the stock footage world, has produced a number of highly profitable clips using live footage composited with animation and effects. One of his more successful examples is a clip of a man on a street with a cell phone. David animated virtual communication waves transmitting into space and around the globe and animated the virtual camera to zoom out from the man to watch it all happen. It took David more than a few days to shoot composite and animate that one clip, but it has generated well north of $10,000 in earnings for him. One clip—over $10,000. Not a bad return.

As proven by Multifocus, when done properly, combining animation and effects with live footage can produce clips that add up to *massive* sales. The downside of this technique, however, is that more often than not, the time, money, and resources spent to produce a clip with effects results in very little, if no financial return at all. In fact, Multifocus himself has many clips that took just as much time to produce as his big winner that haven't sold at all. And I know from firsthand experience that some of the composite clips that Uberstock has invested significant time and money into have proven to be pathetic sellers. Now, that's not to say that a tastefully done lens flare here and there wouldn't be worth the extra work, but I strongly urge you to consider how these time-consuming special effects will affect your overall margin. Spending time and money on effects is the ultimate risk/reward-type play. If you produce a hit, you can make a ton of money. More often than not, however, you'll probably end up striking out.

> SPENDING TIME AND MONEY ON EFFECTS IS THE ULTIMATE RISK/REWARD-TYPE PLAY.

DO SOME GRADING

Color grading, or color correction, is a process that allows you to adjust the contrast, saturation, hue, and tone of your footage. You might do this for two reasons: 1. Because you made a mistake while you were shooting and you need to correct it (like forgetting to white balance or underexposing). 2. Because you want to stylize your footage to make it more unique and/or to deliver your message better. Color is always subjective, but the simplest way to explain the goal of color correction is to ensure that the blacks are black, whites are white, and grays are gray. Skin tones should look natural, so you might turn up the green, turn down red, compensate with blue, or tweak the magenta. If it's supposed to be a happy shot, lighten the blacks and saturate the colors. If what you're after is a shot that represents depression, bump up the contrast and de-saturate the colors.

This critical technique takes a lot of time and practice, but when done correctly, your footage will have the optimal look, feel, and marketability. Again, there are fantastic resources both online and in the bookstore that teach color correction. You don't have to be a pro, but you definitely need to know the basics if you want to make sure your clips will sell.

THIRTEEN

Finishing Strong

CONGRATULATIONS! YOU'VE COME ALL THIS way and now you've got some really strong, sellable clips that are ready for the final stages of the stock production process. These last few steps, however, are some of the MOST IMPORTANT, because without properly uploading and keywording your clips, no one else will find them! So let's talk about how to output, upload, keyword, title and lightbox your footage to maximize visibility.

ENCODING & COMPRESSION

Once you've finished editing, color grading, de-noising, and adding affects, it's time to render your clips and export them in their finished format. Each microstock agency has different requirements for how they want footage encoded, compressed, and uploaded to their site. They ask you to encode your footage properly because that process converts the digital information in your video file to a specific codec (i.e. H.246, ProRes, Photo-JPEG) that is most compatible with their platform. This process may also involve compressing your file, which makes the file size smaller by taking away little bits of information. Study the required specs of each site carefully, then change the settings in your software to compress the footage accordingly. *Always* watch your clips after they've been compressed and *before* you upload to ensure proper playback. There have been many times that a single black frame that was accidentally added to a clip by the compression software resulted in a rejected file from the agency. When that happens, you not only have to go back and fix the problem, but you also lose out on potential sales because your footage takes longer to get back up on the website.

ROBB'S RULES

WHEN ENCODING & COMPRESSING

1. Always watch your clips before and after uploading
2. Compress your footage as little as possible
3. Proper filenaming is critical, organization is key!
4. Choose your own thumbnails
5. Expedite metadata entry using .csv files
6. Review the requirements for each site carefully

The thing to remember with stock footage is that you really want to compress your footage *as little as possible*, if at all. Whoever buys your footage is most likely going to be working with it in an edit, so it's important for your video files to have as much of the original information as possible. Codecs like ProRes and Photo-JPEG are near-lossless, which means they don't strip away as much information from your video file. Your file sizes may be larger, and they may take longer to work with and upload, but your clients will be happier in the long run because of the quality of your footage.

UPLOADING

I'll start this section on uploading by talking about the importance of file naming. If you're in this for the long haul and looking to maximize your profits, organization is absolutely key to being efficient with your time. One shoot can generate forty to fifty video clips at a time, sometimes more. If you are able to produce one shoot a week for a year, then you are looking at over two thousand clips on your hands. You have to keep these files organized in your system, not just with proper folders and labels, but also with the filenames themselves. If you ever have to go back and find a clip, you want the filenames to match or at least be close to what you uploaded to the site. So look up the agency requirements ahead of time and choose a naming convention that will be both uniform and understandable through the uploading process. I can't stress the importance of this step enough. Organization is key.

Now that you've got all of your clips named properly, you can start creating the thumbnail images that will represent each video clip on the site. The filename of the thumbnail should be the same as the clip only with a tag such as "_thumb" at the end. Again, this will help you keep everything organized. But wait, aren't thumbnails automatically generated for you upon upload? Yes! They are. And that's a huge timesaver! BUT this one image is going to represent your entire video clip online. As potential buyers scroll through pages and pages of search results, it's your carefully chosen thumbnail image that plays the key role in making people stop and

> **THERE ARE TIMESAVING MEASURES YOU CAN TAKE TO EXPEDITE THE DATA ENTRY PROCESS.**

click. This is massively important! So are you really going to rely on some computer-generated screen grab to sell your clip, or are you going to take the extra time to make this image count? Think about it, who knows your footage better than you? You should be the one choosing which image best represents your video.

The next step in this process is preparing your clip metadata. Metadata is all that written information that goes on the stock site about your clip: length, title, description, category, keywords, etc. Prepare this data ahead of time because you're going to need it for every clip you upload, and there are timesaving measures you can take to expedite the data entry process. Each stock site is a little different, but most of them accept something called a .csv file. This type of file is created from a spreadsheet (i.e. save as .csv), and it gives the website instructions on how to fill out the metadata fields for you. If you're uploading dozens or even hundreds of clips, this is an absolute must. You can find guidelines on each stock site that will give you specific instructions on how to format your columns in a spreadsheet and what information to include to create a successful .csv file. Then it's as simple as "save as" .csv and upload to the website! Fast, efficient, and it will save you some of your sanity. The alternative (and some sites will force you to do this) is to copy and paste your metadata from the spreadsheet into each field for each clip as you upload.

Once you've named your video clips properly, carefully chosen your thumbnails, and made sure your metadata is written out, you can collect and attach your model releases. Nowadays some sites allow for a master release document (one release form that applies to all your clips from one shoot), but others require you to customize your release documents for each individual clip. Read the release requirements carefully for each site and follow their instructions accordingly. This part of the process can be a pain, but you might as well get it right the first time otherwise you'll be dealing with rejected clips and having to upload missing documents again and again until you finally get it right.

> **THINGS TO REMEMBER:**
> **ASSETS REQUIRED BY ALL STOCK SITES**
> 1. Clip
> 2. Thumbnail image
> 3. Metadata
> 4. Releases

Know that, across the board, all stock sites require these four assets to be uploaded: a clip, a thumbnail image, metadata, and releases. To keep it all straight, I suggest creating a folder for each clip and putting all four files into each folder. It would obviously be so much easier if every stock site structured their uploading process in the exact same way, but they don't. Each process is slightly different, but know that they all require these four assets in one order or another. Familiarize yourself with the different processes and develop your own efficient workflows for batch uploading your clips to various sites.

THE KEYS TO KEYWORDING

This is extremely important. You can film the best clip in the world, but if you don't describe it carefully and completely with your keywords—NO ONE will find it. Some agencies allow fifty keywords; some stock agencies, less. You need to think both BROADLY and SPECIFICALLY about the subject matter in your clip. Ask yourself, what concepts does the clip convey? What is the main subject matter? The general tone? It's vital that you carefully choose the appropriate terms to be sure everyone finds your work.

Overview of Keywording

Keywording is the most important step in the clip information entry process. **The key is to be highly detailed and specific while being broad at the same time.** It's kind of an art, really, so let me share some tips.

First off, and this may seem obvious, you need to make sure your keywords are relevant. Seriously, keyword spammers ruin it for everybody. If your footage is of a man flying a kite in a field, your keywords should *not include* random details like bush, tree, grass, string, cloud, or sky. None of these words are the subject or focus of your shot. Imagine if you were looking for a clip of a bush and when you typed in the keyword you got a clip of a man flying a kite. Irritating, no? And this frustration leads to mistrust and negativity towards the system as a whole. We want to establish trust with our clients so that they can rely on our clips to always be relevant to their searches. I'll tell you how to do this.

ROBB'S RULES

WHEN KEYWORDING:

1. Relevance is key!
2. Trust the search engines
3. No "laundry list" tagging

One of the most surprising things that I've learned over the years is that the search engines on these stock sites are far more powerful than you might imagine. I remember in the beginning sitting down with a thesaurus and trying to think of every possible synonym for every possible word I could squeeze in my fifty-keyword limit. The truth is, though, that's really not necessary anymore. If you choose the keyword "dog," for instance, modern-day intuitive search engines are also going to search for: dogs, doggies, puppies, canines, or man's best friend. So truly, less really is more.

In fact, "laundry list" tagging is simply not an effective strategy for getting traffic to your clips anymore. Generalities dilute search results, and that hurts everybody. I recommend distilling your keywords down to the most specific and relevant topics, then trust that the search engines are going to do their job. It might sound shocking, but fifteen to twenty keywords should really be the max for any one clip you upload. And if you carefully refine your ideas down to these fifteen to twenty words that best represent your clip, the keywords you end with will be better and stronger because you took the extra time to really think about it.

Choose Words Wisely

Start by researching all of the most popular stock footage sites for footage that is similar to what you've just shot. Filter your search results by popularity and look for relevant keywords that are consistently used across all three sites. Jot these down.

If you're still new to the keywording journey, brainstorm more ideas using a list. Now, I want to preface this technique by saying that times have changed. We used to create lists that were as long as they were broad. Today, however, less is more, and as you gain experience you might build up enough intuition to skip this brainstorming process altogether. But for now, I'll walk you through the brainstorming process then tell you how to refine your list.

I suggest creating a living document that you can reference in the future. Start by titling five table columns: **WHO, WHAT, WHEN, WHERE, WHY**. Watch the clip and fill out the columns in as much detail as possible regarding the main subject or activity.

Keyword Brainstorming Chart (with examples)

WHO	WHAT	WHEN	WHERE	WHY
Thin	Running	Midday	Outside	Amusement
Overweight	Laughing	Happy hour	Inside	Relaxing
Beautiful	Playing	Dusk	Industrial building	Fun
Unattractive	Fighting	Afternoon		Party
Sexy	Crying	Golden hour	Park	Entertainment
Woman	Singing	Twilight	School	
Man	Working	Early morning	House	Pleasure
Young Adult	Hugging		Restaurant	Enjoyment
Businessman		Raining	Street	Work
Hipster		Sunny	Farm	Routine
Family		Bright		Errands

- **WHO**: Make sure you include things like age, physical characteristics, and descriptions (thin, skinny, overweight, beautiful, unattractive, sexy, woman, man, young adult), ethnicity etc. What kind of a person is this? Businessman, hipster, model, family? If you were to put them into a category, which one would it be?
- **WHAT**: Describe the action of this clip. What's happening? What is physically or emotionally driving this clip? What action makes this clip different?
- **WHEN**: When does this clip take place? Midday, happy hour, dusk, afternoon, golden hour, twilight, early morning, etc. What is happening because of the WHEN? Is it raining, sunny, bright, etc.?
- **WHERE**: Where is this clip taking place? Outside, inside? What kind of building? What kind of location? What kind of environment? What takes place in this location?

- **WHY:** Why are the people there? Is there an occasion? Are they celebrating? Are they there for amusement, relaxing, fun, a party, entertainment, pleasure, enjoyment, work, routine, errands? Why would they do what they're doing in this clip?

After you've listed this concrete information, make two more columns titled **CONCEPTUAL/THEME** and **KIND OF CLIP**. List the words that apply to these headings.

Keyword Brainstorming Chart (with examples)	
CONCEPTUAL /THEME	KIND OF CLIP
Warmth	Portrait
Innocence	Candid
Conflict	Abstract
Hope	Urban
Disappointment	Lifestyle
	Panorama
	Crowd
	Stylized
	Era
	Modern
	Future
	Classic

- **CONCEPTUAL/THEME:** These are your adjective keywords. What emotions and feelings are being displayed? What is the concept and idea behind this clip? For example, it could be warmth, innocence, conflict, hope, disappointment, or any number of other feeling type words.

- **KIND OF CLIP:** What does this clip represent? Is it a portrait, candid, abstract, urban, lifestyle, panorama, a crowd, stylized, era, modern, future, classic?

Now you have a bunch of potential keywords listed on a page. The hard part is narrowing the list down to the fifteen to twenty words that matter most. So let's sharpen the ax. First things first, are there any keywords on this list that are redundant? Eliminate any and all synonyms—that's what the new and improved search engines do. No need for multiple versions of the same word or idea. Omit plurals and conjugations (i.e. no eye, eyes, eyeballs, etc.).

Now let's talk relevance. Remember, keywords should only describe the central focus of the clip. If there's a man fly-fishing in a river, please do not include water, rocks, rapids, etc. You should also eliminate any words on your list that are too generic. The keyword 'man' is not specific enough for this shot. The same goes for conceptual ideas. The fly fisherman may be feeling 'hopeful' that he'll catch a fish, but that concept is not specific enough to be one of your ten keywords. 'Harmony' might work, if we see him perfectly casting his line back and forth with the movement of the water, but only if that's what you were truly trying to convey with the original shot.

> YOUR KEYWORDS SHOULD BE *CRYSTAL* CLEAR

Again, your keywords should be *crystal* clear. No metaphors, no similes, no obscure or creative language. Your keywords should be very literal, but you should also consider the connotations of words you're using and choose the one that's most representative. For example, footage of a newborn baby being handed to his mother for the first time could be described as 'beautiful' *and* 'adorable', but because of the connotative meanings of these words, 'beautiful' is probably a stronger keyword for this image. Alternatively, footage of a newborn baby in his cap and booties snuggled in a crib is probably more 'adorable'. The point is, just pick one, not both.

If, after all that, you haven't narrowed down your list to twenty words or less, go with your gut. Intuition is a powerful tool, and it will only get stronger with time and practice. If nothing else, remember that you can always change your keywords after the fact. In fact, we've been spending a lot of time ourselves lately going back over old clips and updating the keywords. But take it from me, it's better to get it right the first time!

Connected Through Keywords

It's important that similar clips from the same shoot have the same top three keywords. That way, when someone searches one of ours, all related clips from that shoot will appear in the results. These three keywords should be the most obvious and literal terms out of the lot. Many times they end up being the who, what, and where, but that's not always the case. Keep in mind, though, the relevancy rule still applies, so don't use the keyword on a clip if it doesn't actually apply.

TITLES & DESCRIPTIONS MATTER TOO!

It's important that you take the time to accurately title your clip and provide a good description as well. The title not only gives a potential buyer a better idea of what they will see in the clip, but the words used in both the title and description are also used by some agency search engines to help provide more accurate search results. In other words, they provide context for your search. Here is an example of both a good title and description.

> **Title:** Eggs Benedict
>
> **Description:** Pan across two delicious eggs Benedict with asparagus and garnish
>
> **Why they're good:** The title describes the subject accurately with as few words as possible.

Your title should immediately say the subject of the image in a simple way. Just the basics. And use spaces between words in your title, not underscores. Know that your title will often get cut off in the search results, so keep it short and people will get the gist regardless.

The description elaborates further details of the subject, and refers to a specific camera movement that motivates the shot. Let me emphasize this last point, the movement *motivates* the shot. There's no need to include camera movement in your description unless it's motivating. If you were shooting a soccer game, you wouldn't call out every movement the camera makes to follow the ball. But in this shot of eggs Benedict, the camera movement describes what is happening. And your description should do just that: describe the image subject and contents. Always use succinct, deliberate, and relevant language.

MORE RESOURCES

To help you in the process and to make sure you are entering in the best keywords to maximize the sale of your clip, here are a few different websites you might find useful:

> **ADDITIONAL RESOURCES**
>
> www.rhymezone.com
>
> www.imagekeyworder.com
>
> www.worldmetadata.com
>
> www.arcurs.com/keywording/

LIGHTBOXING 101

Some stock agencies use a term called Lightbox. This is a function that allows you to link your clips to a group of your own similar work, then draw the buyer's attention to those related clips.

The idea is that if a potential buyer clicked on one of your clips, they obviously felt it had potential to fulfill their footage needs. If, after closer inspection, they realize it isn't what they want, you should make every effort possible to show them your other clips in your lightbox that could potentially fill their needs.

For example, you could put all the clips from one shoot in the same lightbox, OR combine all of the clips where you've used the same model. If you've had many different shoots featuring dogs, put them in the same lightbox. You get the picture. However you group your related work, just make sure that you're utilizing this awesome function so you're maximizing your exposure to potential buyers.

FOURTEEN

Optimizing Your Returns

NOW THAT YOU'VE GOT YOUR awesome footage uploaded and ready to sell, let's make the most out of it by developing a promotion plan. Here are some different ways that you can promote your portfolio and increase sales.

MARKETING YOUR FOOTAGE

In theory, as a stock footage producer, you should be able to focus on producing great stock footage that is technically sound, upload, and let the sales and marketing responsibilities fall on the agencies. After all, that's why they keep fifty to eighty-five percent of the revenue from each sale, right? While, technically this is accurate; in reality, it can make a significant difference in sales if you promote your work on your own as well. There are a number of ways to do so, starting with promotion on the site itself.

INTRA-AGENCY PROMOTION

Intra-agency promotion means using every marketing tool you can inside the website of each additional agency. For instance, some agencies allow you to build html links to lightboxes on the viewing page of an individual clip. In this case, if a viewer is looking at your smiling female business owner footage, you could create an html banner on the page that takes the viewer to a lightbox with other female business owner footage. If the clip they are viewing doesn't match what they are looking for, this link gives the potential buyer an opportunity to look at additional footage from YOUR portfolio that might work better for them, rather than some other contributor's collection. Most agencies have developed their websites to help buyers find other footage that's similar to the footage on a current viewing page. They aren't necessarily, however, directing these viewers to YOUR content. If you want to give yourself better odds that this will happen, you have to develop ways to market your collection to viewers within the rules and opportunities of the agency website.

EXTERNAL PROMOTION

Most successful stock footage producers also engage in a fair amount of external marketing and promotion. One of the primary external marketing vehicles is a website. Additional promotion occurs on such social media channels as Facebook and LinkedIn, as well as social video websites, including YouTube.

Your Website

Your website should do a number of things for you. It should help to build both your brand as well as your credibility. It gives you an opportunity to sell custom production or postproduction services to buyers, and it gives you a platform from which you can connect with your customers.

Let's talk about building your credibility and brand. Your website should be a place where any potential buyer can see a good cross section of your work. They should be able to see the type of work you specialize in, the niches you cover, and the quality of footage you produce. These examples will ultimately lead buyers to perceive you and your brand in a certain light. Based on your use of copy, color, images, and videos, they will get a good sense for the type of producer you are and the standards you adhere to in your work. This is brand building. Those potential buyers should also be able to read about your experience and see your professionalism and attention to detail, which ultimately builds your credibility.

ROBB'S RULES

FOR YOUR WEBSITE

1. Display a good cross section of your work
2. The quality represents the standards you adhere to in your work
3. Provide potential buyers with a way to contact you!

Your website should also supply potential buyers with a way to contact you. This is important, because you never know what kind of opportunities may present themselves. For instance, a buyer may want you to shoot assignment work or re-edit some of your footage for an additional fee.

Some producers like to include behind-the-scenes images or footage, instructions for talent, and even a blog section on their website to give buyers an in-depth look at their operation. These elements all help to further connect with your potential customers. Whether you include these is up to you, but they are certainly worth exploring.

YouTube

YouTube is a great platform to not only showcase your work, but also market to potential buyers. If your videos are properly described and keyworded, there is a massive audience that can find your work on what is currently the world's second-largest search engine. And if you use the description section to include links to your portfolio on the agency websites, there is a great opportunity to drive traffic to your library and hopefully increase sales.

Social Media

Again, most successful stock footage producers have a social media presence. Some, like SimonKR, are extremely active in social media, while others are limited users to say the least. Most will admit they don't really see a significant correlation between social media engagement and direct sales, but they all will say that it gives them one more way to stay in contact with their end users and keep their brand top of mind when people are looking for footage to buy. Humans are emotional creatures. That said, all things being equal, if there is an opportunity to buy a clip from someone a buyer has engaged with on Facebook, versus someone they've never heard of, more often than not, they'll buy from the person they know.

Demo Reels

One of the first things you'll want to do to help promote your library is to create a demo reel of your best work. At the very least, you should have a single demo reel with your best footage represented. Some producers like to develop special category demo reels to highlight footage collections of certain subjects. For instance, a producer might have a demo reel with just their holiday footage. You will want to use any and all demo reels on your website, and also put them on your YouTube, Facebook, and any other social media channels you use. Before you start throwing a bunch of footage together with your favorite song, however, there are a few things to keep in mind while developing your demo reels.

First of all, show your best work. Make sure the clips you use have great content but are also composed nicely; communicate a clear feeling, emotion, or concept; and are technically flawless. Viewers understand that your demo reel represents your best work. Make sure you show it to them.

ROBB'S RULES

FOR DEMO REELS

1. Show your best work
2. Brevity is bliss
3. Choose music with care
4. Leave viewers with a call to action
5. Watermark your work

Secondly, keep in mind that brevity is bliss. It's best to keep your reel short. Use ONLY your best stuff, and show only enough of the shot so viewers get a good sense of what the subject is as well as the quality of the footage. Keep the demo moving. It's always better to have a reel that is too short over one that is too long. You want to leave viewers wanting more, not tuning out and leaving the demo because they are bored with the same, redundant content. In a perfect world, you will be able to keep it under two minutes. Ninety seconds is even better.

Next, choose your music with care. Choosing the right track or wrong track can make all the difference in the world. If you choose a tune that is obnoxious and offensive, people aren't going to want to stick around to look at your demo. If it's tiresome and cheesy, they'll probably leave too. Pick something that matches the tone and emotional feel you want to convey through your footage. And, if at all possible, something with a positive vibe. You know, something that would help people to associate positive feelings and emotions with your footage.

I don't know all of the legal ins and outs of copyrighted music, but I do know that I prefer to buy royalty free music for our demo reels. Doing so ensures my video won't get pulled down or muted for copyright infringement. I suggest you do your legal due diligence before choosing any track. That said you'll almost always be safe by paying just a few dollars for a royalty free tune at one of the many online royalty free music services.

In addition to providing your viewers with a great soundtrack, you're also going to want to give them a great call to action at the end. Your call to action should be some sort of instruction to get in contact with you, visit your website, or check out your portfolio on your favorite agency website. At the very least, you should put your name and website URL at the end of the demo reel.

Finally, you will also want to watermark your demo reel. Watermarking is simply the act of placing a semi-transparent logo over your video. This is especially important if you are going to upload the video in high resolution. This watermark not only serves as a constant reminder to viewers as to who's footage they are viewing, but also discourages people from downloading and illegally using your footage in their videos without paying for it.

FIFTEEN

Keep it Going

IN MY CLOSING CHAPTER, I want to take a step back and do my best to project the future of what stock footage may become. At present, I estimate that across the stock footage agencies, nearly ten thousand videos are purchased every day. Despite the increased library size and the increasing numbers of competitors, I have certainly enjoyed reaping the benefits that have come to those fortunate to be in this industry for any extended period of time—I regularly sell as much in one month now as I did in four to six months several years ago. I am also wrapping up several of my most profitable months ever—I continue to see higher revenue, increased traffic counts on my website, and increased referral earnings.

So where do we go from here? Will this growth level off? Will it collapse? What does the broader economy have to say about the growth of microstock—is global economic growth good or bad for contributors to microstock footage libraries? Will one to two dominant video libraries continue to emerge over time and will consolidation sweep through the industry?

As to the immediate future, it appears brighter than ever. I outlined in my first chapter the voracious appetite for motion media that keeps accelerating. There is an ever-increasing market for video content in movies, television shows, webisodes, corporate marketing videos, and any number of other online and offline locations, and they are ALL crying out for good, high-quality stock footage to help fill their runtime.

> It's a great time to be in the stock footage production business.

There is also a strong argument to be made that as production budgets get cut, stock footage will become more and more necessary. As firms continue to thin out their in-house production capabilities, people will be required to move to the lower cost options of producing video content, which will include purchasing stock footage.

It's a great time to be in the stock footage production business. With the right knowledge, experience, practice, and plenty of perseverance, you too can develop a strategy and carry out a successful plan to become a stock footage millionaire.

Acknowledgements

Let me start off by saying that this book has been 4 years in the making. I've had the help and support of many people over the years, and to all of them I owe my sincere appreciation.

First of all, Kirk VanderLeest. You helped me get this book started way back in 2010. My deepest thanks for getting the ball rolling!

To the current Uberstock team: Nick Perkiss, Spencer Hadduck, Seth Whelden and Noel Adams. Nick, you are Uberstock's champion and fearless leader. I not only appreciate all of the time and energy you've put into helping me with this book, your knowledge of the industry and your ambition to stay at the forefront, never cease to impress me. Spencer, you are an integral part of Uberstock, and the ultimate team player. Thank you for owning the "back end" of our production process, and for all of your guidance while writing this book. Seth, thanks for your continued contribution of "cinematographic" talent and tireless ambition. Your thirst for professional and personal growth inspires me. Noel, thank you not only for your DP skills and abilities, but also for helping educate Tracey on our postproduction process so that she could help me keep it all straight.

To the former Uberstock rock stars: Steve Crocker, Colleen Rowley, and Mike and Sean VanSooy. Steve, you are one of the most talented artists I've ever had the pleasure of working with, and owe a lot of our success to your early efforts. Colleen, you took the Uberstock torch and successfully ran with it in the early years before any of us really knew what we were doing. You were not only a fantastic first leader, but also one of our best selling models. As part of the initial Uberstock team, you both deserve credit for being the pioneers who helped build the foundation for what Uberstock is today. And Mike and Sean, you guys played such an important role in our growth as a company. Thank you all.

Jim Pickerell of sellingstock.com, Lee Torrens of microstockdiaries.com, and Andy Goetze of Pond5.com, thank you all for making the time to read and critique the early drafts of this book to help improve the final product.

To Eric Harrison and Zach McIntosh of Nimia. Thanks for taking time to review the book and share with me your future vision of the industry.

To Patrick Lor of Dissolve. Thank you for sharing your insight on the industry and providing a knowledge resource for me and the Uberstock team.

To Jim Goertz and Lon Parker of iStockphoto: A heartfelt thank you to both of you for all your encouragement, guidance, and support in the early years… and for planning and producing all of the amazing Videolypse adventures I was a part of.

Big time thank you to Tom Spota and Derick Rhodes of Shutterstock, for all of your guidance and support this past year, and especially during this writing process. And to Shutterstock's Ben Pfeifer, I'm eternally grateful to you for making things happen.

Thank you to John Neff (aka jjneff) and Keith Jefferies (aka vesperstock) for your colorful and inspiring stories and image contributions.

Shout outs to kick ass interns: Shannon Breen, Andrew Schaffer, Benny Wizansky and Andrew Ruiz. Thank you for all your help from making graphics to scouring back up boxes for old footage. Thanks also to Michael Fitzgerald and Maurissa Fisher for volunteering as models.

To my assistant Tracey Whitney for keeping everything on track, and for being game to help with anything, anytime, while making sure nothing ever fell through the cracks. You are a game-changer for me. This book truly couldn't have been written without you.

To my beautiful girls: Carly, Kenna and Caris, for being the most awesome kids ever and the world's greatest live-in talent. And Dana, my beloved, ever-so-tolerant wife, for (usually) supporting my stock footage endeavors—like letting me bring cameras into the delivery room…twice.

And finally, thanks to the stock footage community of contributors, many of whom have become amazing and life-long friends, especially fellow Stock Footage Millionaires, Simon Krzic (SimonKr), Daniel Hurst (Via Films & MorganL), David Baumber (Multifocus), Luke Miller (Pathos Media & MorganL), Louis LeBlanc (Rebelz), and the dozens of others I've had the pleasure of meeting over the years.

Here's to a long and successful career doing what we love, and loving what we do.

About the Author

© Funnelbox

Robb is an impassioned founder of three different companies, including Uberstock, one of the worlds leading stock footage content providers; Funnelbox Inc., an award winning strategic video agency; and Flixio, an industry leading digital signage content company. He has spent the past 17 years learning how to best help clients, partners, employees and friends reach their best and highest potential … in whatever they decide to do in their life and career.

Robb speaks on the subjects of small business leadership, business video, video strategy, and stock footage production. He has authored *Stock Footage Millionaire* and is currently working on his second book about video strategy for small business.

Robb has directly or indirectly produced and/or directed thousands of videos for organizations large and small including: Nike, HP, Intel, Microsoft, AT&T and Toyota. He is active in YPO, EO and YEC.

Robb lives near Portland, Oregon with his wife, Dana and their three children. He's active in local philanthropic organizations and local government. He loves to golf, maintain his small orchard, and play with his beautiful little girls … and he especially loves helping others reach their best and highest potential through speaking, coaching and encouraging greatness.

Robb's Resources

There are dozens of resources and links to help stock footage producers that I have gathered at: www.stockfootagemillionaire.com/resources.

Bibliography

Jackman, John. *Lighting for Digital Video & Television*, Aug. 1, 2002

Mascelli, Joseph V. *The Five C's of Cinematography: Motion Picture Filming Techniques*, Jun. 1, 1998

StillMotion. KNOW—*Field Guide to Filmaking.* stillmotion.com

Weston, Judith. *Directing Actors: Creating Memorable Performances for Film & Television*, Jul. 1, 1999